Book reviews on th.... .. ..
Browning's earlier books:

'Under Cader Idris' (5 stars)
'A beautifully written novel. The author captures the atmospheric area and the intertwining lives of the people who live there. I thoroughly enjoyed this book and was sorry to finish it. Highly recommended.'

'Come Laughing!' (5 stars)
'Must read! What can I say? This book is amazing. I laughed out loud, frowned, cried, groaned, sighed and cringed, sometimes all at the same time! What a breath of fresh air – feminine honesty and reality at its best. Utterly brilliant!'

'Villa Eden: A Bulgarian Travel Journal' (5 stars)
'Warm, funny and very human: another great book from a writer with a singular wit, and a unique outlook on the world. A small but perfectly formed insight into a time, and a place, and a state of mind.'

'A Cretan Diary: Journey through the Senses'

Alienora Browning worked as a secondary school English teacher for many years. Now retired, and living in the West Country, she is the author of eight other books.

3

Other books by Alienora Browning:

Long-Leggety Beasties

Come Laughing

Riding at the gates of Sixty

My Esoteric Journey

The Lyre of Logres

Booby Fellario's Lockdown Diary

Under Cader Idris

Villa Eden: A Bulgarian Travel Journal

For S, S and A, with love.

Between 2010 and 2015, I was lucky enough to visit the beautiful island of Crete on five separate occasions, with my husband and our son, staying with friends in their wonderful home in the village of Armenoi.

During those five holidays, I wrote regularly in the journal I have kept since 1972 – and this book captures four of the five Cretan adventures through the medium of diary extracts, and photos taken at the time.

Many thanks to our hosts for all kindnesses, sharing of vehicles and expert knowledge of the area.

No real names, or photographs, of friends and family have been used in this book.

PART ONE

Thursday 29th July – Thursday 12th August 2010

Monday 2nd August

We are in Crete, have been since last Thursday. It's an amazing place. The downside is that I have been full of adrenaline, anxiety, aches and pains. It has made me realise how tense and full of foreboding I am all or most of the time. I have been given a book – 'Feeling Good,' all about Cognitive Therapy – and it's got some very positive-looking exercises. I shall use these every day to try and move my cognitive freeze on to a more reduced setting.

As I sit in the lower patio/dining room, I can hear the cicadas scratching away; I can see the hot and dusty hillsides, dotted with trees, the stark white of buildings and the shark-fin peaks of nearby sets of mountains (the White Mountains, Kephali and Kalogravis).

A bell tolls somewhere. So still is the air that sounds carry, light as dreams, clear as a spring, up to us and beyond: Maria, a neighbour, berating cats; when night falls, the starlight barking, and the vicious, creepy moaning howl of tom cats disputing their territories.

Geraniums and fresh basil, in large earthenware pots, line the wall. A hammock swings gently in the breeze.

This is such a lovely place. Prickly pears, we have seen, banana trees, lemons and oranges.

Our hosts have been very welcoming, kind and generous, showing us many of their special places and introducing us to friends, taverna owners and acquaintances.

I confess that I did get myself into a complete state of anxiety before, and during, the flight. I can remember sitting in the Departure Lounge, feeling absolutely terrified and overwhelmed, but not wanting family members to pick up on it.

My throat was dry as we walked out towards the plane. Take-off was alarming, and my head was swimming and felt weird.

We hit a patch of turbulence (over Italy, I think), bad enough for toilets to be closed and us all to have to strap ourselves in – and that did scare me; but, without a doubt, the worst part of it all was my internal monologue, the constant mental chittering – because, actually, most of the time, I was barely aware of the plane's movement, the stewardesses were great and it was a beautiful, hot day.

As we approached Greece, I plucked up the courage to look out of the window – and I am now so glad that I did because it was stunning: sky intensely blue, the deeper blue of the Mediterranean sea – oft-imagined, now seen in reality – the bumpy crusts of coastline, and the whole wonder of this incredibly ancient world/civilisation.

The plane gradually descended over the terraces and fields of Crete, sea so close that we could see the waves.

Boiled sweets really helped the ear-pressure/head chaos. We saw the wings extend to their fullest, felt the wheels lock into readiness – and then we landed, a vast expanse of blue sea to our right, sun high overhead even though it was 7pm local time.

Once we had got our cases, we met up with our hosts, and drove, from Heraklion to Armenoi, in their hired car.

This journey freaked me out. I have never been driven on the right hand side of the road (or at least, not as an adult); the landscape is very hilly with long sweeps of road and vertiginous edges – and it felt as if we were travelling very fast. I started to feel really panicky, unsafe and upset; my whole body was clenched.

The speed fear was, I now think, caused by my misunderstanding of kilometres per hour, and my cretinous assumption that the higher numbers meant we were going faster! I really should have listened during Maths lessons at school.

The sunset was fantastic, though: a band of rose-gold descending sea-wards – you almost expected to hear it hissing and sizzling as it hit the water.

Such a contrast to the muted palettes – and sense of solar reluctance/meanness – one experiences in the UK.

The house, in the hills of Armenoi, is wonderful. It has a patio right at the top, at roof level, with four chairs, a table, and several pale-turquoise dragonfly lanterns.

We tend to congregate up there, once darkness falls, with oregano-flavoured crisps and glasses of Coca Cola, to watch the shooting stars. We can see Scorpio and the Milky Way very clearly.

Back to our arrival: once we had unpacked, the five of us walked down into Armenoi, through narrow alleys and past ancient-looking houses, the scent of jasmine strong in the hot air, the percussive beat of the cicadas a constant.

Crete is very much a taverna society – lovely, I think, both socially and gastronomically. Tavernas dot the countryside. That first night, we went to Operros, a taverna in the village owned by Andreas. The food was/is a revelation: delicious, fragrant, light – salads, vegetables in batter, meat with peppers, chips. We have, thus far, tended towards the sharing of several different dishes routine. This works a treat – and means I get to experience loads of new and different taste sensations.

It is fascinating to possess, and be using, Euros; to see the brightly-coloured bank notes; to have coins so different, so foreign, in my little green purse.

We ended the meal with a speciality of this particular taverna: three flagons of raki (a local wine/spirit – strong booze, basically, with more than a touch of fire-water to it!), one brown, with a cinnamon flavour; one minty green, and, my own personal favourite, a pink, rose-flavoured number! We sampled all three. I only had a tiny taste (as I am still wary of alcohol) – but the rose one was gorgeous.

Puddings came free of charge, and we were presented with a plate of deep-pink slices of water melon – luscious.

That night, I slept badly: the heat; the unfamiliar surroundings; the mosquito net and, I suspect, the bottled-up plane terror crashing upon me. Whatever the reason, I woke feeling agitated and with left arm pain.

Friday morning, we drove down the road to the Late Minoan cemetery. It is fascinating – lots of individual graves, with steps/slopes leading down to them. Many had green-painted pillars. Son saw, and took a photo of, a tiny scorpion in one of them. The final one was huge and very impressive, though I found the heat oppressive and difficult.

We then drove to the Historical Folk Museum at Somata – an eclectic, nay eccentric, collection housed in two rooms situated behind a barn. The owner/collector is a splendid old chap called Vangelis.

He had an extensive beard, a spreading girth – and, due to working in Germany for several years (fairly common in Crete around World War 2), a wonderfully polyglot approach to language. Thus, he introduced his wife as 'Mein frau,' and his conversation was sprinkled with German words.

He was clearly very taken with Son – and they shared a passionate interest in matters military.

He hugged the lad warmly, and they had their photo taken together before we left. Very touching.

One of the graves in the Minoan Cemetery.

The heat rippled, spread; my head felt dreamy, dizzy.

In the afternoon, we had a siesta during the hottest hours, curled up under the mosquito nets, doors and windows open, the aromatic scent of a Cretan heat haze wafting.

Then, as day cooled towards evening, we took a most stunning drive up through the mountains and down to the South Coast, enticing glimpses of bright blue sea around every corner – or so it seemed. The sun was still hot and heavy, almost a physical presence in its own right. Plakias was the name of the town and, from there, we drove to a bay beyond Souda.

A steep flight of stone steps led down to a small beach, rocks on either side, two or three people already in the sea. The water was so clear; it was incredible.

In we went, cold at first, then lovely, and so buoyant too: you could just lie back and float peacefully, lulled by the power of the

West (in magical terms), the siren song of water.

The others went snorkelling. Son was so excited, God love him: he had never done this before – and he really went for it. I could see the tip of his snorkel, bobbing up and down, as he followed our hostess into the deeper areas, near the rocks.

That evening, we drove up to the taverna at the top of the village of Kastellos, just down the road from Armenoi. The owner is a most charismatic guy, called Vassilis. He is very friendly and exuberant, with an excellent sense of humour.

The atmosphere was great. We were out in the courtyard. The moon hung huge in the sky, like a silver breast implant. Peeping from behind trees, it almost seemed as if it were listening in.

The food was delicious. The fact that it was cooked fresh, by Vassilis and his wife - and much of it sourced from animals, herbs and vegetables located in fields adjacent to the taverna - made it even more special.

The atmosphere at this courtyard taverna, high up on the hill, was wonderful – a blend of fabulous smoky cooking smells, night-scented flowers, laughter, and the excitement of dish after dish of new and enticing food to sample and enjoy. Magical, the whole thing.

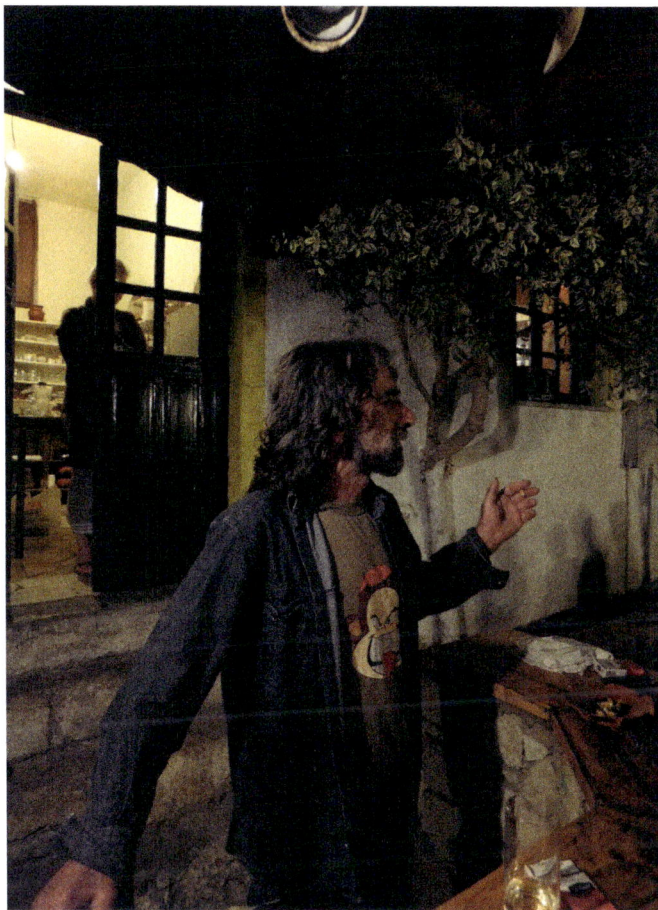

That night – or, to be more precise, early Saturday morning – husband went downstairs to the toilet, banged his head on the low doorway, and staggered into the loo, pouring blood all over hands and floor. He then had to try and hold the wound whilst mopping up the puddles of gore. Fortunately, it wasn't serious, just messy (scalp wounds always bleed a lot).

I knew nothing of this until the next morning – and then felt really guilty because I didn't go and check that he was all right. I was vaguely aware that he had gone to the loo – and he did seem to have been gone for a while; but I just thought, 'This is my anxiety at work again...'

Saturday morning, I felt very anxious once more: the physical agitation; the acute sense of danger; the intense fear of collapse – horrible.

After breakfast, we drove to Rethymno – the nearest city – and visited the mini market. I felt very hot, spaced out and panicky; but, having said that, the produce on offer was pretty amazing: huge tomatoes, aubergines, fresh figs.

Delicious!

Oh! I forgot to mention something important: on the way back through the mountains from Plakias, we stopped at a taverna to watch the sunset – and it was magnificent: pinkish lilac light, like fairy dust, seeped down into the mountain peaks, staining them; it was as if the softening light actually entered the rocks – the whole thing somehow humbling, I guess the reflection that we busy little beings are, actually, pretty insignificant, and that the roseate light shower will outlive us by centuries.

Back to Saturday: later on, we returned to Rethymno, and visited the Fortezza. Up high above the town, sprinkled with pines, it is a fantastic fortress, built by the Venetians in the sixteenth century, and includes a Greek theatre with tiered seating, the stage ready for the next show.

Rethymno, as seen from the Fortezza.

I had an immediate memory of the last time I went to see a Greek play at Bradfield College – and the powerful, haunting production of 'The Trojan Women' we saw that night.

The fact that all the parts were played by schoolboys did not detract from the strength of the performance one iota.

Rethymno Fortezza

It was uncomfortably hot walking around the Fortezza, and I was sweating like a warthog.

I have always had very pale skin – and a touch of the Pre-Raphaelite about my looks – and, with a history of hay-fever, sun-stroke and divers allergies, have long been more comfortable in colder climes. One of my anxieties pre-Crete was that I would come over all unnecessary, and swoon like a Victorian maiden, at the slightest hint of heat.

Having never fainted in my life, the chances of this actually happening were, it has to be said, a tad on the slim side - and, even if I had, knowing my luck, I would have landed on a rotting sheep, or in a large dog turd, and not in the arms of a romantic hero.

Ah well! A girl can but dream. Ditto, a fine figure of several women, of advanced years!

The best bit of the Fortezza for me was the abandoned mosque, with its beautiful tiled ceiling and superb, echoing acoustics. I stood in the centre and performed an

Awen. It sounded amazing – cleared the room! Embarrassed the hell out of my family, I am sure.

There were also two underground tunnels – wide, fairly long, the second one filled with tombstones.

The pine scent, as we walked through the little grove, was intoxicating.

In the museum, I saw several very small, beautifully-decorated sarcophagi. There was also a boar bone/tusk helmet which had, I think, been found at Armenoi's Late Minoan Cemetery.

It always amazes me – when I look at the artefacts left behind by ancient civilisations – how advanced these long-dead people's skills were, and how talented their artisans. You look at the detail, the love, that has gone into a Roman statue, or the Minoan sarcophagi, and it does make you question our twenty-first century assumption that we are superior, more cultured, more anything really.

After our siesta, we drove to Poodle Rock/Petres Beach, a stretch of the North Coast just outside Rethymno. The sea was lovely and warm. The others snorkelled for ages, whilst I lazed and floated and watched the bright golden sun begin to deepen and sink. Warmth surrounded me.

Children's voices cut through the hot, still air. The sea grew darker; the sun's colour display formed into lines of lilac and red, peach and gold and blue. We swam and watched, watched and swam.

Darkness clamped the world. Children still swam. We showered behind a clump of trees, then watched for a bit longer from the courtyard of a taverna above the beach.

Then, in the evening, we walked down to the village and went to Andreas' taverna. Great food again, including a lovely scrambled egg and courgette dish – and an amazing pudding: cheese-filled pastry, with quince jam on top. It worked brilliantly!

I am really impressed by Son's spirit, his kindness, the way he is up for everything: the snorkelling, eating snails, trying internal organs, drinking raki and retsina.

Bless him! He is loving it here.

Yesterday, we drove up through Kastellos to the mountain road, ending up at a super taverna in Argyroupolis.

The setting was beautiful: trees, mountains and gorges. The taverna had a spring roaring and tumbling through it, and the water we drank came directly from this. The sound of the water was so welcome on such a hot day.

Flowers at Argyroupolis.

We met up with John and Sofia, friends of our hosts — and ordered mounds of food. John, who is around seventy and looks like Gerald Durrell, is lovely: English, quietly-spoken, intelligent; Sofia, roughly the same age, is an Ethiopian Greek, and reminds me of Irma Frei, a Browning family friend — a very warm and caring lady.

After this, we walked around Lappa, and saw two most beautiful Greek Orthodox churches, before visiting a necropolis with a church and a huge plane tree, the latter over two thousand years old and now split into two sections. The biggest branch on the left hand tree looks like a chimera: dragon's head, eagle's body, snake's tail.

Part of the necropolis.

The church's name had been hilariously mistranslated as 'Holly Five Virgins' – which gave the whole thing a decidedly pagan feel to it, and made me envisage them as a quintet of arboreal goddesses, related at some level to The Green Man (perhaps spawned by him!), with skin as green as holly, red and gold berries depending from various orifices, and a decided aversion to the procreative act, either through fear or nun-like devotion!

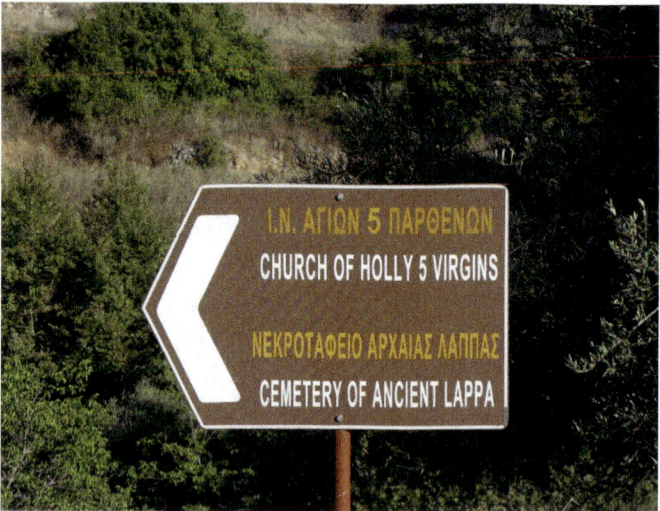

Today has been a quiet day, a day to reflect and catch up, though we are going back to Petres Beach later, and then to Rethymno to visit the Old Town and eat at a taverna.

Wednesday 4th August

A few cicadas are starting up their Mating Overture, the randy little buggers, their little legs rubbing together in a sexual frenzy. Already, at 9.40 am, the heat haze is such that we cannot see the near mountains, let alone the White ones.

A dog barks down below, and we can hear the intermittent loud imprecations of Maria, as she screeches at the local cats or speaks on the phone to relatives, all part of the aural backdrop to our lives here.

Petres Beach on Monday was magical: beautifully warm water; a golden road tracking over the sea's surface to the West; the sun sinking gracefully behind majestic, lilac-shaded mountains; rosy afterglow like a giant pashmina draping the shoulders of the world; sun striking the windows of a house opposite.

Rethymno Old Town at night is amazing: vibrant, colourful, full of noise and bustle and young people. There are these lovely old streets, lined with ancient buildings – a huge mosque, a Venetian fountain, the remains of a Turkish dwelling – and many modern shops, selling a riot of brightly-coloured souvenirs, which stay open until midnight.

One shop amused me hugely, specialising, as it did, in a range of huge, and anatomically-correct, phalluses. The statue at the doorway – revealing its intentions (as it were!) with admirable and thrusting elan – gave way to a most peculiar, and hilarious, world of penis bottle openers, hat stands, erotic playing cards, tooth picks – and, I have no doubt, slightly more pliant models on sale for those times when the swiving partner one so desires is unavailable.

I gave in to temptation, and bought a stonking great membrum virile bottle opener, envisaging the range of wonderfully suggestive moments at social-evenings-to-come, as I yodelled, to my spouse, 'Darling, shall I use the jolly old procreative organ to open the Champers?' or words to that effect - and witnessed the guests rearing back in nauseated horror at the repellent images this conjured up.

As we walked further into this enticing warren of streets, a weird street performer appeared: a living statue, he was very tall, clad in a long, silken white robe, white hat, whited-out face and white gloves. The only colour, two dashes of hectic red against the deathly pallor, came from his lips, and a bunch of flowers he held in one hand. He looked creepy, like a symbol of death and disease. He was completely still, which was unnerving in itself; I could not see his chest rising and falling at all. Tuberculosis in a shroud. Death in life.

After a while, we saw people approaching him, tourists ('touroids' as our host rather splendidly calls them!) and Cretans alike, posing with him, having their photos taken. This normalised him somewhat, took away some of the peculiar mysticism.

We had dinner at Goran's taverna, right in the heart of the Old Town. Goran, and his wife, originally came to Crete from Serbia in the early nineties when the former Yugoslavia's break up and genocidal nightmare was at its bloody and raging worst.

The food was lovely. We had octopus. It tasted like chicken and was delicious, but the tentacles freaked me out a bit. We also had a superb baked tomato and cheese dish, gorgeous mopped up with bread; a Serbian variety of Greek salad, meat balls, kolokythokeftedes - and, to finish, Goran's exquisite and delicate Panne Cotta, drizzled with caramel sauce, the perfect antidote to the highly-spiced and rich savoury dishes.

The atmosphere was so different to a typical drinking evening in the UK. Young people were sitting at tables, in or outside tavernas and cafes, chatting and drinking – but there was no aggression, no rowdiness; there was none of that awful sense of tension and threat you find in Bristol or Weston-super-Mare. It was delightful to see. There was an aliveness, a beauty, a sliver of sweetness and innocence.

Crime statistics are very different on Crete: no hard drugs, little stealing or violence; it's a place where women can walk alone, safely, at 3am. You don't get yobs, or bunches of drink-fuelled youths out looking for trouble.

What a revelation! But also, what a sobering reflection upon the life we accept, and assume to be universal, in our country.

,ɔt, as if it were normal, a level of violence and nastiness which is neither necessary nor life-enhancing. It is so sad, such a waste of the human spirit, that tiny piece of divine spark we all possess. Whether seen as literal, or as a metaphor, it is that part of ourselves which transcends bodily concerns, that has the ability to soar to the dizzying heights of spiritual revelation and artistic inspiration: it is the creative flame.

We walked round the harbour, with its Turkish lighthouse, and Pirate Cruise Ship, the bars and tavernas behind us pumping out music; fluorescent greens, blues and purples striking the ancient stones. The moon, like half a ripe peach, hanging luminously over the harbour; no tide because the Mediterranean is an enclosed sea.

As we strolled, our hosts told us about the tank of foot-nibbling fish lurking in one of the city's back streets. Apparently, this weird therapy is very soothing, gets rid of all manner of gunk and doesn't cost much!

My body seems to be adapting to the flow of life here, the sweep of the roads, the right hand side of the road driving. I feel less panicky when travelling, am relaxing. I have even sipped small glasses of red wine and a tiny smidgen of raki (both shared with Son) the last couple of evenings. The red wine is delightful, to my surprise: it is light, fragrant and has no preservatives, so the heavy hangover feeling is rare.

A trio of golden eagles regularly fly overhead here. We have also seen Alpine swifts, turtle doves, a Scops owl, a lanner falcon and a most gregarious, yet indignant, car-chasing Guinea fowl.

In the sea, the snorkellers have spotted two moray eels, hermit crabs, damsel fish, spider crab, bright-hued wrasse – and divers multi-coloured bastard fish. As one of the party said, it is like having free acupuncture, with tiny bites all over your legs.

We were all just up and doing yesterday, when the phone rang. Andrew and Laura, two artist friends of our hosts, are in the area, and the plan is to catch up with them later today.

Going back a bit: we are only three hundred miles from North Africa here, Libya to be precise. Isn't that amazing? To answer my own question: probably not! But for me, with the geographical knowledge of a bed-pan, mind-blowing.

Andrew and Laura are doing up a wonderful old Cretan house. It is going to have artists' studios and all sorts when completed.

It was very hot when we drove out to see them – well over 30 degrees, probably 34 or 35 – and, once we had helped them unload their possessions, they invited us in for tea/coffee.

The little bit of house they have sorted out so far used to house two hundred and fifty rabbits, and is tiny, like a gipsy caravan, with bright green walls and lots of colour elsewhere. They have built/designed a sleeping platform right at the top. Lovely place; delightful people.

We sat at a table in the courtyard, and near a fig tree. The whole thing has a decidedly Bloomsbury feel to it; to be more precise, it puts me in mind of the Vanessa Bell, Clive Bell, Duncan Grant menage of ragamuffin delight at Charleston, and in the South of France.

They sought the Mediterranean ambience, light and colours as inspiration – and I can now see why: the herby smells in the warm air; seeing figs, pears, olives, apples, prickly pears and pomegranates growing on trees at the side of the road; the intensity and wonder of it all.

We went for a fantastic drive during the middle part of the day. Up into the mountains, we drove, high high up, rocks of white and grey and red, stark and dry, like parts of a skeleton, as if the bones of the land had cracked and scattered far and wide. Breathtaking. Birds soared, high up on the thermals.

We dipped down into greener, lusher, cooler country and came to a gorge walk leading to a high rocky cave/shrine. A tiny white church had been added to the rock face. It looked like a half-shell stuck on. The shrine once celebrated the Mysteries/Hermes, but has been overlaid with the Greek Orthodox tradition.

A fascinating digression here: on Crete, people bring rectangles of tin, inscribed with pictures, and place them on wires/strings in churches/shrines, as a way of asking the patron saint of that particular place for help with a specific problem. So, we saw lots of pictures of legs, eyes and so forth. I suspect that the Shrine of St Anthony dealt with leg problems because there were lots of crutches up there, as well as the leg picture totems.

There was a hugely ancient feeling, powerful and pre-Christian. The welded-on church husk felt strange, not right, as if trying to keep at bay something which cannot, and should not, be contained.

The family just ahead of us (Greek, two little girls and a toddler boy, all with fair/brown hair and blue eyes) walked up the steps and, next thing I knew, the mother had placed a gold censer round the toddler's neck and was encouraging him to kiss the picture of St Anthony.

They went in, and we left them to it. I suspect that the baby had some medical problem, probably limb-related, and the parents were interceding with the saints on his behalf.

As we walked away, I became aware of a presence – green, wild, horned: Pan. He was there for a bit, then vanished.

We drove around the most stunning lake, shining greeny-blue in the hot afternoon sun, then stopped at the village of Thronos, to see the ancient eleventh century church and its magnificent frescoes.

As we approached the church, an old crone appeared. She was the Wielder of the Key, and clearly had some considerable status/influence in the community. She wore a blue and white dress, had long white hair in a bun, and shrewd brown eyes in a seamed face.

Once we had viewed the church, and I had bought five postcards of the frescoes, one for each of us, we went to the village wise woman/witch's cafe.

She had a tiny triangular courtyard at the back. Fragrant with potted herbs (basil and oregano), it looked out, and down, over the most beautiful views. Thronos is very high up – truly a throne overlooking the land, its kingdom.

We stopped a bit later to look at a huge monastery, and saw a monk, clad in the long black robes of the Greek Orthodox religion, getting out of his car. As Son commented, the vehicle seemed wrong, out of place.

Would it have been more in keeping if the monk had rocked up riding a donkey? Or rattled in with horse and cart combination? Or even – dare I say it without being struck by lightning? - in Monty Python, Holy Grail, mode, chanting religious mumbo-jumbo, interspersed with loud crashes as holy book met clerical noggin!

No! Get thee behind me, Shades of Light Comedy! Let the poor man have his car!

The monastery itself had an air of wealth and opulence about it. The monks own a fair bit of land, grow their own grapes – and have a gift shop/taverna/souvenir place to rake in yet more dosh from the touroids. So much for chastity, poverty and obedience! The monastery was at Arkadi.

Finally, and on the way back to Armenoi, we stopped at Skaleta beach, which is to the east of Rethymno, and swam, floated and snorkelled.

In the evening – and after finding a tiny pink gekko in the toilet!* - we drove to Agapi Taverna, which is just round the corner from Poodle Rock, and had a meal with the artist friends mentioned earlier.

*don't remember eating that!

We had a table right by the water's edge, and were surrounded by a motley crew of semi-feral cats and kittens.

Things we ate that I hadn't sampled before: fresh sardines (luscious), and a broad bean, olive and garlic dip, which was delicious.

All very convivial – and the odd fragment of flesh may have slipped under the table, to be enjoyed by the feline gang.

Random Donkey Moment!

Thursday 5th August

Evening of a hot hot (36 degrees) day. The bells in Armenoi toll: the top note is buoyant, but there is a sonorous/ominous undertone. Has someone died? We had, for the most part, a quiet day yesterday – though there was great excitement when

Son found a brown lizard in one of the downstairs rooms – and we all flocked in and took loads of photos, lying on the floor in order to get closer to the little darling! Then a member of the party picked him/her/it up, which opened up all sorts of opportunities for close-ups of the head. It was gently released outside after this Trial by Paparazzi!

Loads of people ride motorbikes in Crete – and almost none of them wear a crash helmet. It seems really weird, dangerous, makes me anxious just looking at them, especially if you see, as I did yesterday, a father with his little boy behind him and his even-littler girl in front, all in shorts, t-shirts, and light shoes, not a crash helmet between them.

The police do crack down from time to time – and, for a while, people wear the gear, or at least carry one with them just in case – but Cretans are not big on rules and, I have to say, the wild, uninhibited, rebellious part of my character (pretty squashed and embryonic these days) rather admires them for this. After all, there are no absolute rules. Laws are a human construct, not a divine one.

I am really having to confront my own fear and repression here – and am looking at all the rigid rules I have created in an attempt to make life feel safer.

Does it work? No.

Another thing I have noticed is the very different – and, in my view, far more sensible and healthy – attitude towards alcohol and drinking. Alcohol is always served with food and water. People don't seem to drink just for the sake of it; it seems to be more a social thing. At every taverna I have been in, the first things to arrive are bread and a bottle of water – and the water is regularly topped up/replaced during the meal. When you get a tot of raki at the end of the evening, there is always water available.

Yet another thing, we have seen some very beautiful old ladies here, particularly in Rethymno Market. Often clad in black – and, thus, widows – they have lovely, dignified faces, and such a variety in terms of racial characteristics/types. I had assumed that all Cretans were olive skinned, brown-eyed and had dark brown or black hair. But I have actually seen a surprisingly large number of blonde/brown haired, blue-eyed people.

There is a very distinctive Cretan profile which stretches back through the millennia to very ancient times: sloping forehead, large and proud nose, heavy jaw; I have seen some splendid examples of the above.

The sun is setting. Panes of gold light deepen on the wall.

I have felt a bit tummyish over the past twenty-four hours. It may be the alcohol – or it could be the fact that my stomach tightens and gets very tense when we drive high up in the mountains, and there is a big scary drop to the right. What a wimp I am!

Going back to yesterday, we went for a lovely swim at the long beach just down the road from Poodle Rock. I absolutely love swimming, floating and just lolling in the

Mediterranean. The water is so clear and clean-looking – and warm too, wonderfully, joyously warm.

In the evening, we walked down to Operros Taverna, for a meal. It was the owner's thirtieth birthday, and lots of his family members were gathered around several tables, celebrating.

The baker's dog (small, long of body, brown soulful eyes, large teats indicating a recent pregnancy and birth) came over when the meat platter arrived, sat at my feet and looked up hopefully.

We had Greek salad, fava, a cheese and chilli dip, a bean concoction, bread, the meat platter and loads of retsina.

In the midst of all this, I went to the loo and encountered two girls, with the classic Cretan profile, dressed, somewhat incongruously, in Tart Mode.

They were in there smoking, with the window open – and the rounder of the two said to me, 'My father – he does not know I smoke! We are not gay!' and giggled.

'Get your drift!' I said. 'I won't say anything. Good luck!' and we exchanged conspiratorial smiles.

Both touching and amusing, this little interchange: just goes to show that some things are universal – who hasn't nipped off to the bog for a crafty fag, after all? - and that hiding our habits from the parental pair is part of the maturational process. Where (I often ask myself) would all that adolescent fun and heart-pounding fear/excitement be if our parents actually allowed us to indulge every whim?

At the end of the meal, we were given three different coloured/flavoured raki containers and a jug full of ice cubes. The idea was to put an ice cube in your raki glass, pour in your choice of pink, green or brown - and then down it in one fell swoop. Cool!

I poured myself a very small amount of the rose-flavoured drink, just enough to stain the rapidly-melting ice cube, and sipped slowly because I had already put away a couple of glasses of retsina, and was well on my way to being bitten by the barn-weasel. Husband and our host got really creative with their drinks. They searched for unbroken ice cubes, and then poured pink raki in the middle of the cube, and green all around it. As a variation on a theme, they put green in the middle and surrounded it with pink. Their slightly-inebriated care and attention to detail was hilarious.

'Irish Gay Liberation Front!' as our hostess said, leaving us all in stitches.

Raki Art, created by husband and host. Most exquisite use of colour and ice, methinks - though the shades of denture-base pink and toilet-cleaner green may have nauseated anyone who was not ripped off his or her mammary glands at the time.

The Birthday Boy sent plates of delicious birthday cake/pudding round to everyone. It was a wonderful concoction of cream and caramel and chocolate, all moist and cold and delectable.

When he came to our table, we sang, 'Happy birthday!'

As we left, I said, 'Goodbye!' to the 'Daddy doesn't know I smoke', girl, and we smiled at one another.

We walked back up the hill to the house, laughing and chattering.

Shots suddenly rang out, rent the still-hot and herby air, then deep male voices sang in traditional Cretan harmony – and this just struck me a being so wonderful, and a million miles away from the UK: men gathered in a courtyard, half way up a village hill, drinking and singing and firing guns into the hot night sky.

Yesterday dawned hot. We decided to drive up into the hills, and over to the South Coast. The temperature was 36/37 – and it was felt that things would be cooler, and more bearable, in the mountains.

Up through Kastellos we drove, and on to Argyroupolis. We stopped opposite a flight of stone steps, leading up to a shrine cave cut into the hillside. The cave itself stretched right back into the rock, a long tunnel with water flowing on the floor. We couldn't see the end of it because it went round the corner.

Although the outer shrine part was overlaid with symbols of the Greek Orthodox Church, there was a strong sense of something powerful and definitely pre-Christian, something crouched and silvery. A spirit of the cave? A being from long, long ago?

By the side of the road, large hunks of meat hung on wire spits and cooked.

We drove down to Asi Gonia, then up through the foothills of the White Mountains. Amazing terrain: stark white; grey stone; patches of gorse; breathtaking views; road winding up and up and up; cloudless blue sky, like an upturned bowl, ahead.

We stopped half way up and got out. It was fantastic. We could hear a goat bleating, a bird calling – and, other than that, absolutely nothing, a great herb-scented silence rolling out over the Cretan mountains.

I got out of the car, and picked warm purple-headed wild thyme.

As we drove on, we saw goats, and flocks of sheep, sheltering under trees from the intense heat.

We reached the highest point and then descended through the Kallikratis Pass: a narrow series of hairpin bends, dropping rapidly down towards sea level.

I felt a certain degree of trepidation, but our driver took it very slowly and carefully and the views were fantastic (if somewhat scary).

There was quite a feeling of exhilaration at times, and a flood of warm relief when we reached the village of Kapsodassos, at the bottom.

The next bit, on the plain and facing the intense blue sky, was lovely: scrubby bushes, goats, dust, the mountains rearing up in the background, sea on our right and a taverna to our left.

Our destination was Frangokastello, a Venetian fort near the sea. Built of honey-coloured stone, and drowsing in the sun, it was a maze of small, ruined rooms.

Castles and forts have long held a fascination for me, and I often pick up vibrations (of mood, emotion, rather than action) from the long-dead owners of these fabulous places, faint ghosts of thought and strong feeling drifting like dust.

Part of Frangokastello.

On a platform by the entrance, a young man sat, under the protection of a parasol, playing the lyra. The acoustics were brilliant – and the guy's deep voice, the plangent sound of the lyra, and the tapping of his foot against wood, filled the whole ancient shell. Hugely atmospheric; strange wild music which could have come from the medieval period – or, indeed, a time out of time.

Pictures formed. I saw the Venetians, armed and ready, looking out to sea; I saw the boat, loaded with fierce and warlike Turks, advancing inexorably. All of this was triggered by the peculiar and fortuitous combination of a dignified young man practising his lyra (and he was extremely good), and the human 'notes' – from a long-distant past, and stored in an ancient sea fort.

Sunday 8th August

I had a difficult day yesterday: basically lack of sleep on Friday night, and a brief resumption of the extreme panic/left arm pain. Horrible while it lasted, but I seem to be through the worst now.

There was an earthquake at 7 this morning. I slept through it, but apparently it was strong enough to cause the shutters to rattle, and for there to be a strange feeling of displacement.

Back to Frangokastello: it was very weird, this feeling of being in two places simultaneously; of hearing/sensing echoes from the past. Music was definitely the link – but then music has always been my key to the wardrobe of the past/Elven lands. Although the tunes played by the lyra player were foreign to me, I felt as if the whole sound were familiar, something heard/experienced way way back.

Afterwards, we went west to Koutelos Beach: lovely bright blue sea, hot sand — but, unfortunately, we weren't able to swim because the cave, previously used for shelter, had been blocked by falling boulders. We had lunch at Manos Taverna. I had stuffed tomato, stuffed pepper, stuffed vine leaves, and Son had the 'special lamb' ie kid! All lovely, and it was great to watch the waves curl and dance in the bright sunshine.

After lunch, we went exploring, to see if swimming were a possibility. We crawled between two rocks and then, having done so, realised that there was no way out, except by going round by the very narrow margin of sand by the sea's edge. Water swept up and over our espadrilles — exhilarating and cooling. We had to run barefoot across the hot hot sand.

We went back along a very bumpy dirt track to the Beach with No Name, and swam/snorkelled for a while. Then it was along the back road to Armenoi, through Fotinos, and past the hilltop church of Agio Pneuma, perched, like a white nipple, right atop the swelling breast of the mountain.

On Friday, we drove to Rethymno, parked near the harbour – and went to get tickets for the Pirate Ship cruise. It was amazing, lovely, soothing.

We sailed east of Rethymno, as far as Platanes. The ship was decorated to look like a pirate galleon, with crossed swords and a piratical costume on the wall, and several treasure chests by the entrance. One crew member was dressed as a pirate. We spent most of the outward journey standing by the rails and looking out to sea.

Eventually, we came to some fantastic rock formations and sea caves, which included a big stone archway.

The boat stopped. A ladder was lowered. People who felt so inclined jumped/dived into the water from the top deck – or, in the case of most of us, crept nervously down the ladder and lowered ourselves gingerly into the deep!

One member of our party, who clearly comes from merman/mermaid stock, was in first and out last, totally at home in this element.

I was much more nervous, I am ashamed to admit – felt overwhelmed by the depth, by a stab of incipient cramp in my left leg, and, I guess, the fear that I could not keep all my metaphorical ducks in a row; that I could not control the situation.

I did get in, however – and did swim for a while, before panicking and grabbing hold of the life belt, until we were allowed back in again!

Our hostess had loaned me a greeny-blue bikini (which, frankly, became me not!) - and, once out of the drink, I lounged around in that for the rest of the journey, going into 'Two Fat Ladies' mode, seasoning comments with, '...don't you think, Clarissa?' and, 'Oh, definitely, Jennifer, definitely!'

It was 38 degrees by the coast today; a mere 34 in/near Armenoi!

Post sea immersion, the five of us drank lashings of Coca Cola (excellent and reviving/refreshing in this climate), ate oregano flavoured crisps – and enjoyed the sun, the bright turquoise sea, the motion of the boat and the glimpses of land: tourist beaches, with their patches of coloured parasols – blue, yellow, green, orange; the National Road; the Fortezza; people sitting and standing at the harbour's edge, waving at us; a blue and white boat, called The Albatross – (Not a good omen: get thee behind me, Ancient Mariner, and thy blood and feather encrusted crossbow; I'll none of thee!) all glazed to a dreamy patina by the sun.

We disembarked, and then made our way to a little fast-food outfit, and had lunch. Gyros, it was called, and infinitely superior to any fast food you get in England. So, we had pork shaved from the gyros (gyre – and possibly gimble, optionally in the wabe!), in proper pitta bread, with onions, tomatoes, chips and thick, sour yogurt. How good is that, eh?

That evening was the Armenoi Festival, something I was really looking forward to.

A few things to explain (or fit in because I forgot them earlier) first: Friday morning, husband and I walked down to the Bakery (next door to Operros), to buy bread – and, tucked under outside chairs, there were five adorable puppies, all snub-nosed and sleepily drowsing in the early sun, all in shades of black-and-white or brown-and-white.

'Ah! That explains the baker's dog's teats!' I said to husband.

Back to the festival, and some background information: there is a two thousand year old dance tradition/technique in Crete. Mainly a male preserve, the dancers link hands or shoulders and dance a series of patterned steps. It is incredibly complicated, and apparently fiendishly difficult. Some of the men will, I gather, suddenly kick up their heels or leap up in the air. Bring it on, I say!

The other fascinating thing is the whole hill country/bandit connection. The mountainous area of Crete is huge. During World War 2, it was the centre of the Resistance, and people hidden up there stayed hidden. For all we know, there may still be pockets of resistance in the rocky heights!

From time to time, men will ride out, armed, and blast road signs with bullets, until the village names are obscured by ragged holes. More than a touch of the Wild West in Crete's mountainous regions, I reckon.

There are Mountain Men: moustachioed ruffians, who swagger around in combat tops, black garb and drive vehicles without number plates. They live in mountain villages, are suspiciously wealthy and have a reputation for banditry: steal ATMs, for example - allegedly!

The Cretan male traditional costume is very distinctive, and I first saw a photo of a man wearing it on a gravestone. It consists of a black, long-sleeved shirt, beige jodhpurs and long black boots worn over the jodhpurs.

Back to the festival: at 10pm, we walked down to the area next to one of the local tavernas, and met up with the artists. The food was disappointing (meat on a stick and oven chips).

A bit later, the musicians appeared. There was a guitarist, two bouzouki players – and the leader of the outfit, the lyra player.

They were very good, very loud. Gradually, a Cretan circle of dancers formed, and we watched, fascinated.

Not a good night's sleep, unfortunately: I heard the cock crowing the dawn – and, though I guess I must have fallen asleep eventually, it can only have been for an hour or two.

In the morning, we drove up into the mountains, and visited the cave in Melidoni, Gerontospilios. I was feeling very shaky and physically timid – a real shame because normally I adore caves. My legs were trembling – and walking down the steps seemed to take forever. I felt about two hundred years old.

The actual cave was pretty impressive – but the sense of terror, of absolute absence of safety, of doom, was incredibly strong. I was reluctant to go in, felt as if I could easily fall; there was a feeling of threat, a chill.

In 1824, the whole village entered the cave to hide from Turkish invaders. Tragically, the villagers were found. The Turks lit a fire in the mouth of the cave. Three hundred and seventy civilians and thirty soldiers were smothered by smoke. Martyrs. Awful.

In the large cavern, there is a white ossuary containing the martyrs' bones.

I am not sure whether it was my mood colouring things, or me picking up a resonance, a strong vibration, as I do from time to time – but I definitely felt something very powerful and scary.

We drove on, and came to another, much more extensive, cave at Zoniana. There, we joined a guided tour, clattering along metal walkways, six million years' worth of stalagmites and stalactites forming peculiar and impressive shapes, all lit by red, green, purple and white lights. There was no sense of horror or terror, just great age: patience and wisdom, I suppose – something almost unimaginably ancient watching the tiny, short-lived ants that we are scurrying and twittering about.

By the time the stalactites grow another centimetre, we'll be long gone – even Son! The world keeps evolving, keeps shifting and growing, advancing and retreating –

and we, tiny microbes in the vast folds of its skin, just get squashed and re-absorbed.

Friday morning, I woke to the sound of Armenoi's Greek Orthodox priest chanting and singing, as he conducted the service. It was a fabulous sound, deep and mellow, ringing out up the hill.

Saturday night, we drove to Platanes, and met John and Sofia at The White Lady, a touristy-type taverna that hosts both Cretan dancing and belly-dancing.

It was very loud, and things took a while to get going; but, once they did, it was absolutely brilliant, enormous fun.

Manolis is the star of the show. He is a professional dancer. He is also a very good actor, comedian and all-round-entertainer – and he seems like a thoroughly good egg.

There were three main performers: Manolis and another man (both quite short; both clad in the traditional black shirt, jodhpurs and black boots), and a tall, slim woman (wearing a long skirt, top and headscarf/hat).

We could hear the music starting as the three of them got into position, then Manolis whistled very loudly – and they were off. It was hugely impressive: skilled, precise, full of life – and harking back to this ancient and proud tradition.

Right from the start, audience participation was absolutely de rigueur – and, very quickly, our hostess, Husband, Son and I were plucked from our seats by the woman.

We were taught a very basic step (probably mastered in utero by the average Cretan family member!) - and then we linked hands/shoulders and danced all around the taverna, the circle growing as more people joined in, out onto the pavement and back in again. It was great fun: we were all laughing, trying to keep to the beat, trying to remember the pitifully-few steps: a real hoot!

In the second act, Manolis did his comedy routine, in which he staggered about carrying a bottle of red wine and pretending to be drunk. He would lurch into the audience, falling into ladies' laps, feeding men with the wine, often attempting to insert the bottle up a nostril. It was hilarious!

For the third act, Manolis chose about ten men and boys, and got them sitting on the floor in a circle. Husband was one of them. Manolis was wearing a hat – and, after a bit of clever and comedic hoofing, he placed a glass of red wine on the floor, went (well, fell actually!) into the press-up position, picked the glass up in his teeth and quaffed the red wine. This was obviously his challenge!

He then walked around the circle – and, each time, placed the hat upon a random man's head. The two men would then square up to one another, and do a kind of in your face, mock-fighting, cock-swaggering strut. Manolis would perform a complicated dance step, and the other man would have to try and copy it.

At the end of each round, the man chosen had to try and drink a small plastic cup of red wine from the prone position.

Husband's turn came, and he capered most satisfactorily opposite Manolis. He even attempted – with some success, I have to say!- a dance step that would have had me in traction for a year. He got down on the floor and downed his mini-spittoon of wine with no trouble.

It was then the girls' turn (in some cases, stretching the word 'girl' as far as it will go without twanging into 'crone'!). A table was placed in the centre, with Manolis standing on top. Women were extracted from the audience, and placed in a circle round the table. I was one of them, with Son as my steward/companion. Each woman then had to get up on the table, and dance with Manolis.

Poor old Son! Embarrassment by Parents or what?! Character-building, I am sure; but, when you are in your tender pre-teen years, and prickly teens, the last thing you want is the parental pair cavorting in tavernas, dancing wildly and, indeed, getting drunk.

I was slightly worried that I wouldn't be able to climb onto the table, or that it would collapse under my weight – but all was fine, and I had a highly entertaining prance with, or at least opposite, Manolis.

The owner of the taverna is very proud of his country and its traditions, and does everything in his power to promote, and keep alive, the culture. I think that is wonderful.

Once Manolis and company had finished, the belly dancer came on. She was excellent, did a really impressive sword dance. I was one of four women invited up to dance with her – made a total pig's ear of it, of course, but it was great fun anyway.

Altogether, a superb evening.

Monday 9th August

Yesterday, we went to lunch, with John and Sofia, at a taverna overlooking Lake Kournas: beautiful setting. We saw a couple of lizards on the wall, and electric-blue dragonflies skimming near the taverna. There were pedaloes on the lake, but we did not have time to investigate them.

It was immensely hot, and I felt somewhat under the weather.

We went for a swim at Poodle Rock, just before sunset. The sea was rough, waves breaking under and over us. I got a sudden stomach/bowel pain (the olive oil doing its thing? The figs? The heat?), which spoiled my enjoyment somewhat. But the sunset was red-orange and splendid, spreading its candy-pink light over the mountaintops.

My left thigh aches, legacy (pun intended!) of the cave tension and all that dancing in The White Lady.

Wednesday 11th August

Something I forgot to mention: on Saturday, we drove past traditional charcoal burners. Absolutely fascinating: black mounds, with smoke issuing from vents – and that wonderful, evocative smell in the hot, still air. It is a twenty-four hour job – and we saw little lean-tos, each with a bed, on the side of the road, begrimed men keeping an eye on the charcoal.

Monday evening, we had a barbecue to say farewell to the artists, who flew back to the UK yesterday. It was a lovely meal. We set up two tables on the patio, and made various delicious salads: beetroot and garlic; tzatziki; tomato and basil; lettuce and other greens. We also had brown bread and cheese ready.

The men had been shopping early, and had bought seven big fresh bream. Host and Husband put the barbecue together, and lit it — and soon that wonderful smoky smell was wafting up the hill/slope at the front of the house.

All of the dragonfly lanterns were taken up to the deck, and lit.

The artists arrived at eight, bringing potato salad, more tzatziki and a bean salad with them. We all went up onto the deck, chatted, drank and watched the sky.

Then the men put the bream on the barbecue.

We flocked down to the patio, and started on the salads. It was all very convivial and funny, a lovely atmosphere. The bream was delicious. Son decided to conduct a mini-autopsy on his fish (as you do!), paying particular attention to the cranial vault and all that lived therein. Quite stomach-churning actually!

We all sampled the red wine, and the raki. Actually, it turned into a bit of a raki-tasting session. Our hosts had three different varieties: normal, cherry and apricot. The apricot looked like a urine specimen, though it smelt lovely – but the cherry looked like small testicles in blood (not to put too fine a point upon it!), as there were cherries (or possibly gonads!) floating in it.

The stars came out. The talk wound down. The artists went home.

Tuesday, our host drove the artists to Rethymno Bus Station, so that they could catch the bus to Chania Airport.

At around 2pm, we set off for the Eleftherna Archaeological site. Originally, it was an Iron Age fort. It has also been part of the Byzantine culture, the Classical Greek one (600 BC), the Roman – and went right up to the Turkish Occupation.

What is incredible, though, is how unspoilt the place is. It has none of the tat and fuss one associates with sites of historical/archaeological interest in England. It is currently the height of the tourist season – and we saw two other people! There were no safety features, no leaflets; you could just wander around, see what was there – and let your own imagination fill in the gaps.

The whole thing was an acropolis. It wound through rough paths, flanked by two-thousand-year-old olive trees. A fabulous place for a fort: a narrow isthmus, easy to defend, sheer drop on either side and a view for miles all around.

Oh God, it was hot, though, almost unbearably so. I have not yet adapted to the Mediterranean walking pace, more's the pity. Dread scenarios kept the anxiety bubbling at full heat.

We came to a pair of Roman cisterns cut deep, and far back, into the rock – and then slithered down a rocky slope, and came upon this enormous, dark space: vast pillars, some surfaces still bearing traces of plaster, and, most magical of all, a slit in the rock at one end through which rays of bright sun streamed, a series of steps leading up to the light source.

Son stood on a lower rock. The sun rays lit upon him. The red of his shirt bled into, and suffused, the pale gold so that, briefly, he stood out, godlike, a mandorla of gold-red surrounding him – and the light behind him took on the intense scarlet hue. He held his arms out, and blood-coloured brightness rippled through his sleeves and out onto the rocks. He climbed the steps and stood at the top, turned to one side, this time like an Egyptian deity.

Husband and our host took photos. The light faded. The moment was gone.

A bit further on, we came to a cave with a very low entrance. We all had to crouch down for the first few feet. When we stood up, we were in a tunnel, with a lower channel cut into the bottom. It was the overflow from the Roman cisterns. People had written their names on the walls, going back to the seventeen hundreds (though I am sure there were earlier examples); there were rock formations like an octopus' skeleton hanging down:

'An Octopus' Garden in the sun!' as Husband put it. I had had exactly the same thought, complete with Beatles' tune, seconds earlier.

We came to the sun-bleached remains of a basilica, bits of mosaic still visible – and a grave containing two tiny skulls, a pelvis and various other small bones, all at least two thousand years old. I felt very moved by this.

On the drive back, we saw loads of red and yellow dragonflies, hovering above the fences.

Wednesday, we went beach-hopping. Nervousness about the flight had set in, and I was also upset because of my fear of snorkelling, so I wasn't very happy or communicative during our first two ports of call. I wish I could break these frozen silences, by squeaking or chatting or crying – but I become mute, which makes things worse. It can be misconstrued by others, who think me snobbish or cold – instead of scared.

We drove over the Kourtaliotiko Gorge. Nick-named The Hairdryer, it is spectacular. We swam first at Skinaria – beautiful sea, very hot sand; Hostess and Son found an octopus when snorkelling. Host and I, by contrast, found ourselves swimming next to a small, dead wrasse.

We then went to Preveli, Monks Bridge – a wonderful old bridge with large pictorial inscriptions on both sides. A small pond/lake, in front of a taverna, completed the scene – and, as we wandered down to the water's edge, we saw lots of stunning red dragonflies skimming just above the cool surface.

We had lunch at Agia Fotini (a taverna right by the sea), and then the others snorkelled. I tried, but got all panicky every time I put my head under water. I felt a complete failure and was thinking, 'I am useless, no fun at all.'

A low moment indeed.

But then we drove on to Triopetra, a long, surfy beach – and frolicked in the sea, playing with the body boards. That was brilliant fun. I'd never done it before, and wasn't scared at all. It was really liberating. Son and I got washed up onto the hard little pebbles, like so much flotsam and jetsam. Joyous and hilarious.

Gorgeous pebbles, there were, green and pinky-white, lovely when washed by warm waves.

It was then time to go back to Armenoi via the road between Mt Sidherotas (The Iron), and Mt Kedros (Cedar Mountain) and Spili village (Fountains).

We saw some amazing pale green rock formations on the way back, amidst the splashes of almost-Devonian red rock, the grey and the white.

In the evening (our final one: very sad), we went to Kastellos and Vassilis' taverna. I felt mournful saying goodbye to Vassilis. He is a real character.

Thursday morning, we took a final trip to Poodle Rock. The sea was perfect: clear, calm, intensely blue-green, warm. Husband and Son came up to me and said they'd love to help me snorkel. I was very touched by this. So I borrowed Host's snorkelling equipment – like me, he is short-sighted, and has prescription lenses in his mask! - and, with the 'boys' holding my hands, and providing encouragement, set off into the unknown.

Initially, I was very nervous and uncertain – but, once I got the hang of it, the whole thing was great, really exhilarating actually. I could see little fish swimming near me, a hermit crab and the rocks, tufted with sea vegetation; I could see Husband's and Son's legs waving about in the water. It was a peaceful, sun-dappled world down there and, as I got more confident, I began to feel more like a sea creature myself, more flowing, buffeted by the grace of the sea.

Everyone was very pleased for me – and I felt proud of myself.

We went for lunch at Operros, and had a lovely selection of the (mainly) vegetarian starters we have come to love so much over the past two weeks: Greek salad, fava, chilli cheese, dolmades, kolokeft...(er, courgette and cheese balls, basically: after two weeks, I am still unable to pronounce, let alone spell, the buggers!), fried aubergine, tiny piquant meat balls, and the inevitable small jug of raki at the end.

As a gastronomic aside: apparently, and at one of the tavernas we didn't visit

(Agamemnon's?), one of the items on the menu actually is – wait for it! - bollocks! History doesn't relate who, or what, they belonged to. Could be goat gonads, badger balls, ram roistering-sacs.

After our bollock-free repast, we climbed up the hill through the hot, hot sun – and did the final bits of packing. Then a last walk up the dusty, rocky slope, past the prickly pear trees, past the oak tree, looking back down over the house (hundreds of years old, in places) and the mountains.

Our hosts drove us to Heraklion, and the airport: a beautiful drive, though I was tense for parts of it.

After an hour or so's wait, we were taken, by the little bus, out to the plane. The tarmac and air were both very hot; the vast expanses of sea sparkled bright blue in front of us, and the sun was setting over the mountains.

We walked up the steps at the back of the plane, and sat down, Son by the window. The Captain explained which way we were going, and a bit about the conditions.

I was very tense and nervous. It took me about an hour and a half to calm down – but, having said that, I made sure I looked out of the window as much as possible when we took off, and it was beautiful, so dramatic and colourful: bands of colour on the horizon, as the sun slipped into the west, a deep red, orange, gold, and then the vast clarity of the Cretan night sky approaching fast.

The sea was so smooth-looking as we flew over it, climbing higher and higher, the giant wing flaps creaking out to aid the ascent. A perfect silver crescent of moon appeared against the darkening sky – and then, we were up so high, nearly six miles, the Captain told us, that all we could see was curiously bubbly and muddy-looking cloud.

As we approached Bristol, the landscape looked like dark masses lit up by millions of golden Christmas tree lights. We landed ahead of schedule.

What a fabulous holiday it was. Son is a lovely golden-brown colour; Husband is brown pretty much all over; even I have caught the sun on arms, face and neck: amazing!

PART TWO

Tuesday 9th August - Tuesday 23rd August 2011

Thursday 11th August

Wind raked and rampaged last night; shutters rattled; cool air seeped into the room. This morning, the sky is grey and cloudy; a light rain has been and gone. The mountains look faintly forbidding in this light. The cicadas are silent, but I can hear the odd bird call. Despite the general dryness of the greenery, a riot of pink and white and lilac-blue flowers proliferate upon bushes and trees.

Yesterday was hot and dry, 30 degrees, but windy too, so deceptive. We drove, along beautiful mountain roads, smelling of Cretan herbs, pockets of decay and sun, to Plakias. At one point, we twisted and turned through a lovely gorge, rocky ledges almost meeting, clumps of purple gorse breaking up the grey scree. The sea shone, a vivid blue, from every viewpoint, or so it seemed.

We stopped at a high point, parked and admired the view. An eagle hovered, dipped behind rocks, was lost to view. We walked down a dusty track, to a tiny Greek Orthodox church, whitewashed, simple, traditionally tiled upon the roof to keep out the rain. Inside, it was lovely: a bare niche (apart, that is, for a large wooden crucifix) in the East; the other walls studded with paintings of St George, Jesus, Mary.

An interesting thing: women are not allowed in the Eastern, most sacred, space. This seemed strange to me coming, as I do, from a tradition where priests and priestesses have equal weight and validity.

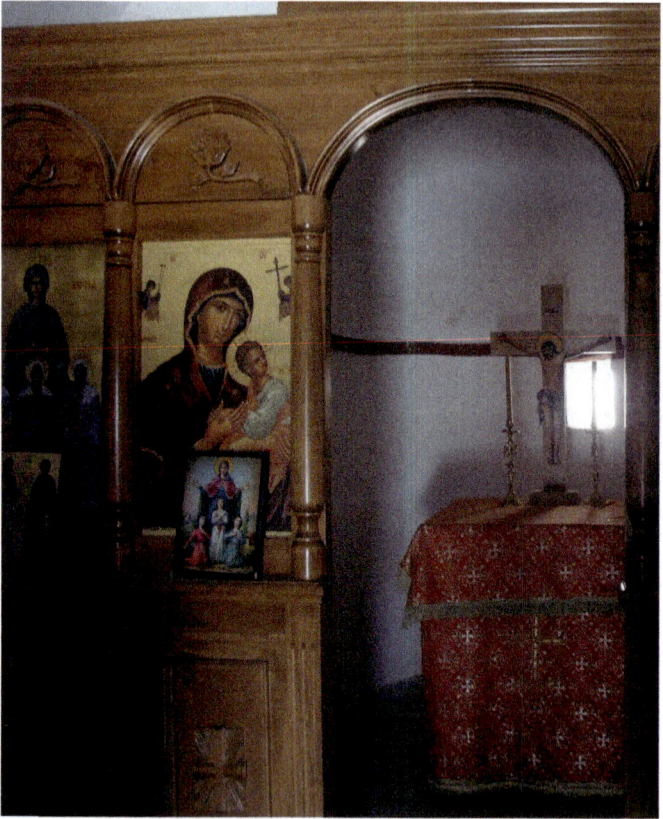

But in a sense, all religions are one – so I faced each wall in turn, and saluted the Archangels, then Hostess, Son and I each lit a yellow candle.

Lily bulbs, some huge like exotic fruit, lay at the sides of the path: strange.

We had lunch in a taverna. It looked out over the sea, the cliffs – and, to the right, terraces and orchards. There were multiple bowls of salad, and you could choose any combination. They all looked delicious, and so bright and colourful, like jewels. I piled my plate with potato and carrot, feta, pepper and mixed vegetables, all drizzled with loads of olive oil and eaten with lovely brown bread. Gorgeous! Host and Husband went for the salad option too, while Hostess had a Greek version of ratatouille (very tasty). Son had dolmades with yogurt, and a very garlicky tzatziki. We ended the meal with raki.

A while later, we drove to the beach. Nudists sported their bits in front of us. I was all for joining them, would have been quite happy to get my kit off (despite boobs down to my waist, and a backside with more sag in it than a knackered mattress), but I could see Son blanching at the very thought of his elderly mother making that much of a tit (all puns intended) of herself.

At this point, I was wearing my new pink Crocs – a mistake, as it turned out. We started to walk along the sand to the sea. Son found a pretty shell, and gave it to me, bless him. The sand was hot, then very hot, then excruciating like some ghastly form of torture. My soles felt as if they had been immersed in a vat of acid. It was horrible. I panicked because the sea seemed miles away, and I could see no way out of the situation. I cried out.

Hostess put a large towel down, so that I could stand without pain; I then put on the pink beach shoes I wore last year, and ran (like an elderly and somewhat decrepit gazelle) to the delectable coolth of the sea.

Ah! That first wash of water over my poor baked extremities! Almost orgasmic in its intensity, my dears! The sea, warm as blood, lulled and soothed me. I floated...

Pausing in my narrative, I note that the sky has lifted and lightened; the cicadas are now rubbing and creaking away as if making up for lost time. I am glad, because I love the sound; to me, it is such an integral part of this lovely place.

Back to yesterday's fiery beach: the five of us bobbed about in the sea, letting the waves push us in towards the shore line. A few broke over my head, filling nose, eyes, throat with stinging salt water – a childhood feeling, that shock but laughter too.

Eventually we emerged, and went on a cliff walk to dry off. The idea was to explore some caves. Unfortunately, I went into panic mode half way along (vertigo?) and Hostess had to hold my hand. I didn't make it to the caves, felt very sad and scared and a total failure.

Up till that point, I hadn't felt much fear: the car journey was great – and, later, I snorkelled at Poodle Rock.

What I do notice is this: a perceived failure, or anxiety jolt, saps my confidence hugely, and I tend to find that I am then overwhelmed by terror. The journey from Plakias to Poodle Rock was difficult for me: I was very tense and frightened.

This is such a shame because, going back to our journey to Crete, I actually enjoyed the vast majority of the flight. It was a warm and sunny day – and, although I was a bit nervous, 'twas as nothing compared to last year.

Take-off was brilliant, exciting. The sky was very blue, clouds pristine white – and the view was magnificent: we could see Venice, the Normandy Beaches, bits of the Dalmatian Coast, the mountains of Greece and then, as deep red bled into the peachy evening sky, the lights of Crete appeared, the Mediterranean got ever closer so that we could see waves upon the silky surface, and we landed upon the rocky landscape of Heraklion Airport.

There were a couple of instances of minor turbulence, but I managed to 'ride' them with only a small jolt of the heart and internal organs.

I read Stephen Fry's 'Paperweight' for much of the flight – and, because it is both clever and funny, that kept me entertained.

The fear of turbulence (in every sense) seems an apt metaphor for my life. But there isn't always going to be turbulence. In terms of the amygdala, I regularly defend myself needlessly. I quiver and hide from a big black monster, which either doesn't exist at all, or is far less formidable when faced head-on. Ninety per cent of the time, the bogeyman I am so frightened of is my own fear grossly distorted.

So, we drove to Rethymno and out, down the Atlantic Highway, to lovely Poodle Rock. Again, delightfully warm sea, the poodle actually quite a handsome and regal beast in the bright early-evening light.

The beach was busy, vibrant: Cretan families, with lots of small, noisy children, paddled and swam. We went out near the rocks, and snorkelled. I borrowed Host's ideal-for-the-short-sighted gear – and, despite a few trembling moments, got the mask on and was under the water pretty quickly. I was proud of myself, despite inhaling a few mouthfuls of sea water.

Everything was so clear, lines of rainbow-hued light radiating out, limpets cosying up in the sand at the bottom. I wasn't brave enough to venture out with the others this time, but have decided to go for it next time.

This, for me, is big progress!

As I said to Hostess yesterday, 'It must be lovely to live without fear!'

Whilst we four were cavorting about in the brine, Host was on the taverna's terrace above, setting up his cameras for the evening sunset.

We emerged from our watery womb, born again in a tingling of salt, and made for the two outside showers. There's something magical about an al fresco spray of cold water cascading down the cleavage.

As we got on to the terrace, a young man appeared, with a string of freshly-caught fish over one shoulder, their scales gleaming in the dying sun. We ordered bream and bass, with Greek salad, bread, dolmades and stuffed courgette leaves — oh, and chips!

The sun sank lower and lower, throwing out rich sheets of gold and apricot; the sea darkened, though threads of colour rippled along its edges.

The fish had been caught using a speargun. They were crisply delicious.

We watched, drinking raki, as the colours deepened to a rich red lined with lilac. We saw the lights of a plane, headed for Chania, as it turned round and positioned itself for landing.

On Tuesday, our plane got in at 8.50 pm local time — and, by the time the luggage carousel had worked its magic, we actually met up with our hosts at 9.20. We then went straight to Kastellos and had dinner at Vassilis' taverna: delightful food, though I was really too tired to do it justice.

The figs have got things moving (if you catch my somewhat unwholesome drift)...

Fear is not failure – and I am not a failure just because I feel fear.

I have borrowed, and am reading, a fascinating, if harrowing, book called 'Eleni', by a Greek-American journalist, now in his seventies, called Nicholas Gage. It concerns his search for the facts surrounding, and people involved in, his mother's death in 1948.

His mother, the eponymous Eleni, was one of a group of villagers from the Greek village, Lia, to be captured, tortured, imprisoned and, eventually, shot. Ghastly.

At present (and I am only on page 19), the forty year old Nicholas is chasing up leads on the whereabouts of guerrillas still alive in and around Athens.

Friday 12th August

Beautiful sunset behind the mountains opposite Armenoi. The five of us gathered on the deck for a good old gawp.

The moon is nearly full; in fact, tomorrow we should be going to a Full Moon Party, organised by Vassilis, somewhere in/near Kastellos. Apparently, it's in a grove of trees, which sounds very magical and Druid-like to me. I am really looking forward to it.

Visitors arrived – and we all walked up the hill to a lovely little taverna: wonderful views, great food, the nearly-full moon dancing with whitening clouds, and a magnificent sunset spreading its palette of colours over the sea.

Sunday 13th August: Full Moon

It was hot when we went to Rethymno Market this morning, but is now pleasantly breezy and sunny.

Pockets of unease/disquiet assail me. Part of it is a resurgence of my long-held belief that I am fundamentally boring: too quiet; lacking the breadth of experience others have; a poor conversationalist.

The Full Moon party is off. Politics, basically.

Rethymno Market

Yesterday, we went on a long, and lovely, drive through the mountainous regions. I adore that kind of landscape, find something both inspiring and consoling about it.

We drove towards the Amari Valley and Psiloritis, the highest mountain on Crete. We went past lovely little fields, dotted with ancient olive trees; sheep and goats, their bells clanking, grazed in the fragrant air.

A week ago, a fierce forest fire swept through fourteen kilometres of the hilly landscape. A wasteland confronted us. In places, the charcoal smell was very strong.

Trees, black and burned hollow, assumed orc-like shapes, lurked like something from Middle Earth by the side of the road. In some areas, the fire had missed patches, so you had the healthy green bits interspersed with black and desolate scapes.

Olive trees are tough and have a massive capacity for regeneration. Later on, outside a little church, we saw a very old one (at least two thousand years old) which had split into six quite separate trees, and was so big that we were all able to stand in its central section quite comfortably in order to have our photos taken.

We found a delightful bridge, stopped and walked over it. To the left was a fig tree; ahead was a carob bush, the pods, like mummified bats' ears, dark and sweet-smelling.

We came upon a stream, thickly decorated with green algae – and, upon rocks and twigs, many dragonflies – crimson, yellow and turquoise-green. They shone, living jewels in the bright Cretan sun.

We visited three little Orthodox churches, one with the ancient and beautiful remains of once-magnificent frescoes.

Driving up the mountain passes was fantastic, the colours sublime: green, grey, lilac, orange and yellow – and, as the sun began to descend, pink and apricot hues began to blend in and spread out. The scent of the wild herbs; the noise of the cicadas (one of which flew into the car and nestled by Husband's foot for a while!); the peace and wonder of it all; the birds soaring high overhead; the turquoise radiance of sea – all of these caught in my throat in an almost tearful gasp/gulp.

I picked various wild herbs, sage and mint mainly, and have started a new Ali's Pocket in my handbag. It should last months, and will be a constant reminder of Crete.

Things fly into the car regularly, it seems: the other day, a Cretan hornet – huge black thing, with yellow spots! - breezed in and lurked underneath Host's seat for a few seconds. Oddly enough, we found another one, in a plant pot on the little balcony outside the front bedroom.

At four, we stopped at a taverna high up. It had a wonderful view of the beige folds, black-green 'skirt' and cloudy halo of Psiloritis.

The wind was strong, great gusts rattling the car and causing hats to blow off. Plumes of greenery, hanging down from a tree behind the taverna, danced like children round a Maypole.

We ordered Greek salad, souvlakis and chips. Bread came with the salad, delicious dipped into the tomato/olive/oil/herb remnants.

Outside, on the square fronting the taverna, there was a plinth with the bust of a local lawyer on it, and a rather striking war memorial: white stone, with a black figure of a soldier and then names/dates underneath.

We also, later on, found a little shop which sold many items made out of olive wood. I bought a big hair ornament (in an attempt to tame the Alienora bush!) for five Euros – and the little chap who owned the place (and who had sacrificed at least two fingers to his art!) polished it for me with olive oil.

We came upon another little pond/stream, again with the lovely blue dragonflies. This time, we saw a fresh-water crab (very rare in Crete, apparently) and several small trout.

The other main monument we came to see was a huge ruin of a basilica. It must have been amazing when complete – was pretty impressive as it was!

At one point, we investigated a very basic road (Potholes r Us, or what!). On several occasions, the four of us had to get out and walk! We saw bunches of grapes on the sides of the 'road', so we picked several and then wandered along in the sun, eating grapes and laughing.

I forgot to mention: on Thursday, at around midnight, we drove up to Castello taverna, to see it if was still open (it wasn't), and a rat darted across the road.

'There goes the Shrine Rat!' Hostess called.

Story behind that somewhat gnomic utterance: our hosts had rats in the roof, caught the little buggers in a humane trap and then transported each and every one to pastures new. One was dropped off in Kastellos; another is starting a new life in or around Heraklion – as you do!

Monday 15th August

Lovely morning: blue sky, hot, slight breeze gently agitating the swimming costumes drying upon the line; cicadas shagging away fit to bust; a rooster proudly announcing to us that day is breaking – at 11.30 am! Clearly a rooster at the end of a very long queue (fowl not being renowned for their intellectual powers) when brains were being handed out by the Great Chicken Deity!

We had a quiet day on Saturday because we were going to Somatas, for their Full Moon Festival, and knew it was going to be a late night/early morning.

At five, or thereabouts, we drove to Petres Beach, where the sea was warm and choppy. We had a fantastic time, floating about and being swept up and into the shore by the undulating waves. They were like sinuous mermaids flexing their abdominal muscles, we the flotsam and jetsam being caught up and discarded, caught up and rolled off, minuscule irritants barely noticed.

Then, clad in beach wraps, Hostess and I went beach-combing whilst the sun dried us off. We found several shells, some sea glass and a tiny cuttlefish bone. Just right for a hummingbird!

I love the buoyancy, the freedom, of warm water; I love floating on my back and watching the hills opposite the cafe, as the sun goes down: magical!

The cats here are very different to English ones. They have sharply-etched, Egyptian features, and are long and skinny. On Saturday, the actual night of the Full Moon, they were out in force, lurking by the bins, yowling, their suspicious watchful eyes following us.

The food at the Somatas Moon Festival was good, much better than last year's Armenoi Festival. We had the usual Greek salad and brown bread, a very toothsome tzatziki, chips, stuffed courgette flowers, and various cuts of meat: chicken, pork and cuttlefish.

The Moon wandered, a giant glaucomic eye, above us; the band played energetically, lovely Cretan music making my feet tap and my soul soar. It started with two of the Maestro's students playing. The better, by far, was a thirteen year old boy, whose lyra playing was, to me, mesmerising. He made the instrument sing, and brought out something of the essential colour and flavour of Crete.

People got up and danced Homer's Circle dance. They were decorous, somewhat inhibited, initially – but it was lovely to watch anyway. The Cretan Circle dance has nineteen steps and is incredibly complex – although really good dancers, like Manolis, make it look easy. Most Cretan children go to dance classes to learn the national dance.

I think that's lovely, a really bonding experience. It would be great if we had something like that in Wrington: the village that dances together, stays together! Hmm! That lost a certain something in translation!

We left at around 2am.

Tuesday 16th August

Very hot this morning: haze over the sky's usual blue – and, again, the image of the blind eye comes to mind. There is a slight breeze. Total silence from the neighbouring cats and dogs (all of whom have been exceedingly vocal during the nights of the full moon!), but the cicadas are frotting merrily away.

As we drove home from Poodle Rock on Sunday, the moon — huge, low, golden — suddenly emerged, as if bowing regally to the setting sun, a giant lollipop waiting to be licked.

We had a quiet day yesterday because we knew we'd have a late night at the Koumi Festival.

I put my contact lenses in successfully (only took about five minutes — damn good going for me!) before we went to Poodle Rock at 6pm.

The sun shone upon the water, causing ripples of gold, as I walked along the shoreline beach-combing. I found some lovely little shells, and added them to my collection of precious things. New theory: Gollum was on the Autistic Spectrum somewhere; it would explain a hell of a lot! He was probably also whelped under the sign of Capricorn!

I felt very peaceful and relaxed and well, as if the salt water were having a restorative effect upon my body and soul.

A deep gold pathway formed over the sea, and I imagined mysterious sea creatures using it to transport themselves from one realm to another. The blue of the sea, and the gold of the sun's descent, put me in mind of the colours I associate with Atlantis. I think there is raw magic at the in-between times, the gaps between fading and brightening, darkening, becoming: doorways open; entities beckon.

The five of us sat at the end table of the cafe's terrace, and watched as the sun deepened to first peach, and then a shade like raspberry sorbet.

A beautiful ginger cat befriended us. It pawed gently at Son's lap, then rolled over on its back and allowed him to tickle its tummy. After that, it jumped onto Hostess' knee, closed its eyes – and appeared to go into an ecstatic trance. Its fur, exquisitely striped, was much rougher than an English cat's, more like a dog's – and it had long limbs and the wonderfully-sculpted Egyptian feline head.

Again, as we drove home, the moon rose, so that it felt as if we were caught between the solar red flare and the paler, cooler lunar orb.

After a quick shower, we drove down the hill to Armenoi – and, when John and Sofia arrived, went in convoy to Koumi - steep roads with hills to our right, and the moon sailing gracefully to our left.

The festival was held in the church grounds. Tables were set up on two levels, an upper one next to the church, where we sat, and a lower one which contained the stage and the band (drummer, two bouzouki players in lilac shirts and the star, the lyra player, clad all in black).

They were very different to the Somatas mob. This lot had long hair; two had moustaches you could have lost a mountain goat in – and there was something wild and passionate about them. Their music was fantastic – and the dancing, when it came, far better than the somewhat Jane Austen-esque shuffling we saw at Somatas.

As we arrived, I saw an astonishing figure – a real Mountain Man: longish grey hair, tied with a grey band; grey beard and moustache; handsome face; black shirt, black leather waistcoat and black Cretan jodhpurs, with black knee-length boots. He was very striking, a good dancer too – though not as good as a younger, very tall, chap.

The latter was superb, almost in the Manolis class, and did all the complicated

leaps, foot slaps and so forth – looked as if he were gliding on a warm current of air, and perhaps in a sense he was. Maybe one of the marks of genius is the ability to somehow transcend the medium in which we habitually move; to touch a more rarefied realm; to slip between the portals.

Before the first – male – circle dance started, a very sweet little girl (maybe two? Three?) took to the floor and danced, by herself, in big circles. She was wearing a dress made of sea-coloured bands, and held a soft toy under one arm as she danced: lovely!

I was intrigued by Mountain Man. He was rather splendid – and exactly the way I have always imagined Nostromo, the eponymous hero of Joseph Conrad's novel; but he was too aware of his own beauty and potency for my liking. There was something watchful, calculating and feline about him.

Hostess and I eventually took to the dance floor – a concrete expanse surrounded by fully-laden tables. The idea was for us to pose in front of Mountain Man/Nostromo – but, unfortunately, I was stone-cold sober, and felt as graceful as a troupe of flat-footed rhinoceri (strong resemblance noted by the audience, no doubt!), whilst Hostess whirled and twirled in balletic mode.

Eventually, and perhaps inevitably, I banged into a table, knocking everybody's drinks over, and crashed to the stone floor, banging my right buttock as I hit the deck. Ignominious or what! I felt utterly humiliated. Definitely not one of my finer moments. A bloke helped me to my feet, no doubt giving himself a hernia in the process.

I seem to have the knack of trying too hard, going base over apex (usually literally), and making a complete and utter mammary gland of myself whenever I am trying to show off in front of a good-looking bloke!

Ah well! Nostromo was nothing more than rather gorgeous eye-candy. I felt no connection at all, nor any genuine desire to get to know him.

Vinegar slathered on my battered rear end should, with any luck, ease things a tad.

Wednesday 17th August

Pretty damn hot today – 29 degrees – but there is a breeze, thank God. My vinegarannointed gluteus maximus feels better: still a bit sore, but not throbbing the way it was directly after my little contretemps with table and stone floor.

Yesterday, we went to Poodle Rock early evening and, having bought a black snorkelling set from the Inka supermarket in Armenoi, all five of us masked up and swam over near the rocks. The sea, though choppy, was lovely and warm.

I was anxious initially, both by how far out I had gone and by the presence of a spear-gunner in full wetsuit. Frankly, the bugger didn't exactly inspire confidence: his first act upon getting kitted up was to fall, in a sprawl of tangled arms, legs – and, more ominously, gun – off the rocks; and I thought to myself, 'With that level of physical coordination, his chances of actually hitting a fish are nil; he's more likely to take one of us out or stab himself!'

But, actually breathing through the tube regulated my tendency to hyper-ventilate – and the underwater world opened so enticingly in front of me that I relaxed, dove down and followed the others sub aqua.

Spread like a starfish, albeit a very large one, atop the sea's surface, I looked down at the rocky continent beneath me: Rainbow wrasse, emerald and turquoise; little yellow fish; many others I could not identify, but enjoyed none-the-less – and, all the time, the waves' undulation bounced me up and down very slightly.

I pause, orient myself, for I am writing this in Armenoi's kafeneio, at around 3.30 pm, and thinking about the kindness and generosity of relative strangers in this warm and lovely land.

Manolis, the kafeneio's owner, gave me a bag of the herbs he uses to make tea – and which I tasted with utter delight; they seemed to create an infusion of Crete itself.

I am actually quite tipsy, after three glasses of raki – most unlike me!

I was writing in here and Manolis called out, 'Some postcards?' - and, when I said, 'No, I write a journal!' he beckoned me over to the counter, and instructed me in some of the esoteric arts of Cretan cookery: brought out a plate full of hunks of mutton, squeezed lemon juice, poured salt – and, lo and behold, a feast fit for a King/Queen. I could almost see that old sheep, eight to ten years of age, wandering contentedly amidst the rocks, the herbs, the hot sun.

Then Manolis poured us both water and a shot of raki, and I tasted the meat and drank the alcohol – all right, I'll admit I didn't down it in one, the way you're supposed to, probably sipped it more like an elderly maiden aunt sprung from

Calvinist stock; but, for me to be under the affluence of incohol at all – well, stap me vitals!

Manolis next brought out the snails and a dish of olives and another of sardines. By this time, all five of us were gathered round the counter. I passed on the snails, but the sardines were delectable. Cheese appeared, and little rusks, and boiled potatoes drizzled with salt, lemon, oregano and olive oil – there's tidy, as we used to say in Aberystwyth circles!

Now, sitting at a table in the kafeneio, head slightly befuddled by the unaccustomed raki infusion, I am writing once more. A great, convivial atmosphere, with the sun outside, and the vines and a cascade of onions curling down the wall opposite.

Where was I? Does it matter? Caught it in the frail and deceptive net of memory — given that people's individual recollections of the same event are so very different: yes, I truly snorkelled for ages, though I missed the flat fish (couldn't distinguish it from its surroundings!) and the moray eel, the latter because the new mask's mouthpiece was deuced uncomfortable after a while, and I ripped it out before it lacerated the inside of my mouth.

But, I did it! I did it! I did it! I have faced that particular fear, and overcome it – pretty much.

The sunset initially looked pale, washed-out – but, as we crested the hill and looked down upon the sea in Rethymno, the colours deepened and gained both height and majesty, becoming a long band of raspberry bordered by lilac: quite extraordinary, nature's tapestry, woven of sun and sea and magic.

Am I a coward? Probably. My immediate, gut reaction is, 'Yes, because I am scared of so many things - and people, come to that.'

My response to driving, to snorkelling, to heights, to speed: all of it, to my mind, shows craven cowardliness and a fundamental weakness of character. Depressing, really. I often feel left out when around bolder, more adventurous, braver people - as if I lack spirit and personality.

We walked the narrow streets of Rethymno Old Town and it was as colourful, bewitching and vibrant as ever – little snapshots of local produce, which included a shop selling shirts.

Son spotted the perfect one for him: black, with a signpost, pocked with pretend bullet holes (as in Bandit Country!), saying 'Crete' and the Greek equivalent underneath.

I had long entertained a fantasy about wearing harem pants – and, finding a shop which had them, went in and tried a pair on. Hmm! I looked like a pig in a colourful sack, and gave that idea up forthwith.

Saturday 20th August

Yesterday was fabulous, utterly magical – particularly given the slump I experienced on Thursday. Friday was windy, cooler, such a relief after the turgid air of Thursday –

but, initially, I was incredibly anxious and agitated.

We drove up the lovely mountain road, sun-warmed herb smells wafting in through open windows, sheep and goats appearing occasionally by roadsides or in the little scrubby fields.

We came to the beach at Preveli, and made our way to the taverna. A great flight of honey-coloured stone steps were cut into the cliff, overlooking azure sea dusted with silver sparkles. The wind picked up as we drank Coke, beer, lemonade and ate lemon-sprinkled grouper (little fish, freshly caught) – delicious.

I began to relax. Originally we were going to do the cliff walk, but the wind was so strong that we felt it would be an unpleasant experience; so we drove on, up mountain roads, stopping eventually by a beach between Preveli and Fotini.

Hidden by towels, we changed into our swimming gear, slathered on sun cream and went for a most refreshing swim. I floated on my back, and looked up at the intense blue of the sky.

As we picked our way down past the rocks onto the beach, a sudden dervish of sand whirled crazily, catching the vulnerable skin our bodies presented: backs of legs, arms.

It was a mad and hilarious moment. Laughing hysterically, peppered by stinging granules, we threw ourselves into the water.

After this, we drove on, the car's motion, the windy warmth and the stunning views soothing my nervous tension – until we reached the beach and taverna at Fotini. The five of us sat down at a table a few yards from the sea.

A tail of multi-coloured cliff curled round the wide expanse of sea, as if protecting it, chunks of grey and orange and green shading the lilac of higher slopes, more distant hills.

We ordered lunch: Greek salad, bread, artichokes, tzatziki, sardines, more grouper and chips. Gorgeous. A dragonfly performed aeronautical stunts to our right while, in front of us, four or five young men took it in turns to dive into the sea from rocks. The draco-curves of Triopetra shone pale and sinuous on the horizon.

We swam and snorkelled at Fotini. This time, I plunged in without fear – and the world under the water opened up before me, huge and clear and utterly magical. Schools of tiny fish swam by; I saw more of the beautiful peacock wrasse, and a large mother-of-pearl shell.

I lay upon the surface, floating gently, occasionally paddling slowly, and let the mask regulate my breathing, sun warm on the exposed parts of my body: such a peaceful feeling.

Time slows down when one is relaxed. The experience above has made me acknowledge how tense I usually am, how rarely I am able to genuinely relax – and how lovely a feeling it is.

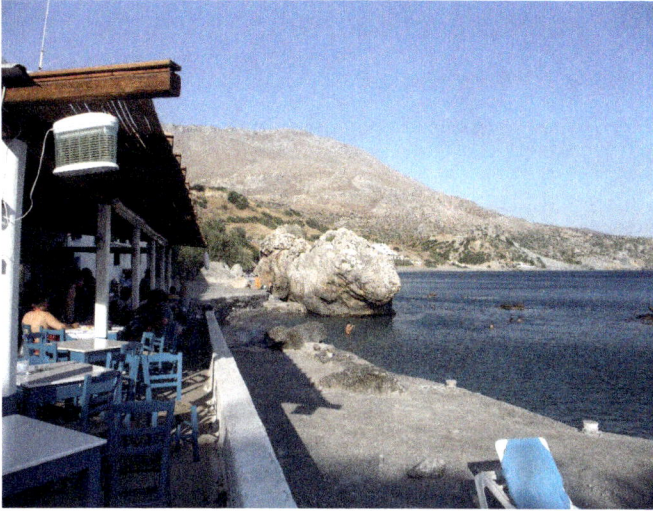

Water is a very healing element. Perhaps this harks back to the time when we all floated gently in our mothers' wombs, our little limbs flexing in the cramped space, sensing that we were safe and protected, and warm and loved.

It may also be that, in the water, we have nothing to prove: that, hair corkscrewed by salt, and limbs in functional mode, the endless, unspoken, dry-land, 'Who is the fairest of us all?' - screeched particularly loudly amongst women – becomes muted by water's amniotic echo; becomes little more than a memory of dark times before slipping beneath the surface.

The sad times, when confidence flees away – and I call myself all manner of unpleasant names - are balanced by sublime moments like the above: spaces out of time, during which I can allow my salt-water-suspended body to simply let go; can let the need to be like others (strong and brave, or beautiful and 'normal') float away with the gentle rhythm of the sea; can let my feet flicker like tiny darting fish; can feel, in that blessed, sun-warmed state, the sacred silence, a loosening of tension and a flowing towards a form of peace.

And I remind myself that there are worse things than lacking high levels of courage; that sometimes the pauses, and emotions, between words are just as important as the long conversations.

On we drove. The wind curled and creaked upon the sea's surface, producing spindrift and misty galloping creatures. We came upon a little harbour, boats tethered and rocking, wind-blown sea dancing.

A few minutes later, as we rounded a bend in the road, a sand/dust storm hit us full on. The windows were closed (otherwise we would have been wearing it!); but the dust, bearing particles of rock, hit the car with great force so that, briefly, we were blinded in a beige and clamorous light: very weird.

We stopped, for a third swim, at the Bay of Triopetra. This time, we were attacked from both sides, and couldn't stop laughing. The sand and dust stung at us, so we took refuge in the water, only to be hit by stinging spray.

The sea, though bollock-witheringly cold at first, seemed warm and cosy in comparison to the forces of nature without. I felt as if I had been flayed after that little lot.

We got changed, with many a merry quip, behind the car, and then motored on home through layers of beautiful sunset-coloured dragon clouds.

A perfect day.

This morning, early, Husband walked down to the bakery and bought two plates full of delicacies: a twist (or, as I called it, a dog turd) of spinach and cheese pastry (lush), three cheese and chocolate pastries and three cheese and honey ones. I didn't try the chocolate one (am avoiding chocolate where possible), but the cheese and honey efforts were toothsome in the extreme – the whole set off superbly by a fresh fig: keeps you regular, don't you know?

Today is very windy. We are off to Mili shortly.

Later:

It is now evening, cool and breezy, and we are back at the kafeneio, opposite S's taverna, on Armenoi's main street. An hour or so ago, a fusillade of shots could be heard, then a hyena-like pack of car horns – a wedding being celebrated somewhere in the vicinity! And, actually, this rings a bell because, earlier, as we came into Rethymno via a back road – stunning hill-top view! - we passed a church and could hear the deep tones of the Priest as he sang his responses to the ceremony. That was rather wonderful.

It was extremely hot, drainingly so, in Rethymno. We parked at the Marina and, fortunately, found a shop selling CDs of Cretan music fairly quickly.

Mili was a fascinating place: a village, abandoned by time and people back in the thirties, and then relocated to New Mili on a hill overlooking the valley/gorge of Old Mili. Great stones fell upon the roofs of houses, and it was felt to be too dangerous for the inhabitants to stay. So, festooned by decades of greenery, these old abandoned houses stand, in some cases only just, a mute testament to the richness and variety of lives lived out in their stone shells.

We walked a ragged path amidst the ruins. The only place intact and still lived in/worked in is the taverna – but, there is no road to it, so supplies are delivered by way of a funicular, a steel cable over the gorge and a little car which carries rubbish out and beer in!

We wandered up white-edged, broad steps to a little church set into the rock of the hillside. Once again, I got the sense of Christianity bolted on, as it were, at a later date – and it may well be that rituals relating to a much earlier set of beliefs took place on that spot. I would not be in the least bit surprised.

There is nothing wrong with this adaptation per se; in fact, it seems eminently sensible, and an excellent way of using ancient things rather than letting them go to waste, wrack and ruin. What does concern me is the human tendency to despise the belief system/s that came first; to label them as evil and ungodly; to assume that Christianity is the apotheosis of all religious thought and practice. No. It isn't.

Soon after this, we happened upon a beautiful glen. It reminded me of St

Nectan's, in Cornwall. I thought it would be a fabulous place for a ritual, and am quite sure I am not the first person to have that particular thought. It certainly seemed like a sacred space.

As I made my tremulous way down the somewhat jagged, and intimidating incline, something banged quite hard against my back. Later, I discovered that it had been a ripe mulberry. Rocks nearby were stained, as if by blood, with the juice.

We went off-piste, in a manner of speaking, and found ourselves, ably led by Son, scrambling up steep and precarious banks. Interestingly, I rediscovered my inner goat at around this time and, helped by good advice (and a strong hand) from Son, was the second person up.

We had a delightful lunch in the taverna on our way back up the path. The wine was a wonderful deep tawny colour, tasted like sherry and went down a treat. Admittedly, I only had a small sip of it (and, later, of the raki), but it struck me as a damn good little vintage. We ordered several dishes of mezze.

Later: I am itching. Mosquitoes? I did spray myself before coming out, but the little bastards have obviously sneaked in while I wasn't looking.

We did not swim today. It was too windy. Great white waves could be seen as we drove along the sea front at Rethymno.

Sunday 21st August

A lovely day. I woke early, for me – by 9am! The weather was warm and breezy.

After a light breakfast of fruit and bread and honey (oh! And freshly-squeezed orange juice: how could I forget?!), Hostess and I set off on a three kilometre walk. I suppose you would have to say round the block – but like no block I have ever traversed in the UK.

We were followed by a most engaging and friendly puppy. It clearly wanted to come with us – and curled itself round our ankles imploringly, wagging its tail and doing the whole wide-eyed bit.

We walked down to a very attractive place meant to be used for festivals and the like. It is much nicer than the square next to S's taverna – but, due to the vagaries of village politics, has never actually been used.

The little dog was still with us at this point. Then its mother appeared, looking anxious – and, a few moments later, the owner hove into view.

It was pretty hot by this time, and much of the walk was uphill, so we rested regularly under shady trees. We saw a green lizard, lots of butterflies, a black bumblebee and various birds. The wonderful aroma of Cretan herbs was all around.

We came, eventually, to the road – and walked along the side of that for a while, then turned up past the vet's to the back of Armenoi. We passed some lovely old Venetian houses – and, lo and behold, came out on the road just above Hostess' abode.

At 1.30, we met John and Sofia outside Inka – and then drove, in convoy, to Iphigenia's taverna out along the mountain road. It was a lovely drive, but I was somewhat preoccupied: my contact lenses were playing up something chronic, and I could barely see.

When we got to Iphigenia's, two more of our hosts' friends – Martin and Maria – were already in situ, playing tabouli at a table. We put two tables together, and the nine of us sat down.

At this point, I nipped off, fairly snappily, to the loo. Both contact lenses were wedged up in the corner and, thus, neither use nor ornament, so I hoicked the bloody things out, bathed my poor streaming eyes in tepid water and rejoined the others, much restored.

The food was not as good as usual, in my view anyway, because there was too much meat. I can, however, now say that I have tried goat (and very nice it was too). We did have some lovely horta, with olive oil and lemon juice, and some exquisite horta-and-tomato fried doodahs, which I absolutely adored.

Last night, at the kafeneio, Manolis brought out a wonderful old wine, ten years old at least, smooth and gorgeous. I drank that, and another variety, and some raki – and, to cut a long story short, Son and I had to help one another up the hill at the end of the evening, as we were both a tad bladdered!

Today, I just joined in with everyone else, and was quaffing the red wine (a beautiful raspberry shade) like a professional, though I had a lot of water and passed on the raki!

After the meal – damn good value: 73 Euros for the nine of us, 8.50 Euros per person! - and kissing Martin and Maria farewell, the rest of us, feeling the lure of something sweet, drove back to Armenoi, parked near Inka and crossed the road to the bakery.

We were presented with display case after display case of enticing goodies. My embargo on chocolate went straight out of the window, and I chose a lurid cream-centred cakey thing, with chocolate on the top. Host and Husband chose Baklava – and received slabs of the stuff the approximate size of the Balkans: they needed serious digging equipment to get it anywhere near their laughing gear.

The girl serving us, though large in the bosom department, was, I think, a little lacking upstairs: she totally failed to give us four of the coffees we ordered (which didn't worry me in the slightest as I never drink the stuff!), and gave me two of the luscious cakes (bargain!). We also got seven patisserie-related objects free!

The seven of us had a great time, laughing and joking and eating (obviously).

I felt quite mournful when it came to saying farewell to John and Sofia, as I have become fond of them. I can only hope that we will return at some point, and meet with them once more.

We drove back home, changed into swimming gear, grabbed the body boards (just in case), and set off for Poodle Rock.

The sea was very rough, with big white waves – not suitable for body boarding or snorkelling. So, some of us went for a swim.

It was wild, man! Very warm, very choppy water, though calmer the further out we got, with great waves knocking us over. It was brilliant, actually, quite exhilarating, though a little bit scary at times.

The sunset was very special, with mountain tops of dusky rose and deep lilac. A large wedding was taking place as we drove back, and both sides of the road were pretty much blocked by parked cars.

Monday 22nd August

Delightful day at the South Coast (for future reference, Poodle Rock is on the North Coast!). A hot day, it was (32 degrees) - though there was, fortunately, a breeze.

We set off up the lovely mountain roads, the smell of warm scented herbs wafting in through open windows; the multi-coloured rocks (now red, now grey, now green) commanding my attention; the sheer breadth of this mountainous glory lifting my spirits.

Signs for Argyroupolis appeared – and, with memories of this fabulous place from last year, we asked to stop there.

Two giant* sturgeon, imprisoned in a small tank, squeezed up against the glass, mouths agape. They looked as if they were gasping for release, or crying for help. By the side of the tanks, for there were two, an elderly man was turning the round meat spit, with the fire underneath it, and the great hunks of dead animal were rotating slowly.

*Actually, they were small by sturgeonesque standards, but far too big for their tank.

Walking down to the taverna, we saw fists full of little unripe bananas. The springs, aquatic falls and luscious greenery provided a little oasis, and the sound of rushing water was welcome indeed.

Lyra music (with bouzouki accompaniment) played in the background, but was hard to hear against the rhythm of the water, the Undines' song.

We had Coke and Fanta lemon, and respite from sun, and dry, though beautiful, craggy landscape. A landscape which is, to my mind, a banquet for the senses, a sensual journey. It encircles the waist with a warm arm, and arouses body and mind with lavender and salt water, thyme and additive-free wine, wild music and flights of lammergeier against an impossibly-blue sky. It soothes and inspires – and brings tears of absolute joy and overflowing emotion.

Up, and up again, we went, wending ever higher, until we veered off even the unbeaten track – having paused, at the wind-swept summit, for me to collect the purple-flowering and fragrant wild thyme – to a rough and bouncing cicatrice in the earth. Son collected several spent ammunition cases.

Suddenly, at the rocky heights, we saw the flash of wings – and two magnificent lammergeier (raptors with a wing span some nine feet in length!) curled up, through eddies of air, into the intense still blue of the sky.

It was an intensely moving experience, watching the regal flight of these rare creatures – a real privilege.

Other birds seen during our holiday: a black kite, red-rumped swallows, honey buzzards, red-backed shrike, stone chats, golden eagles, hooded crows, eagles and gryphon vultures.

PART THREE

June 14th – June 24th 2014

This journal sequence differs from the previous two, in that I decided to do away with specific dates – and the resulting piece is much more impressionistic than the ones for 2010 and 2011. We were also joined by Son's friend, J.

Driving along the National Road at one in the morning, windows down, and that distinctive smell of warm wild herbs, we passed great bushes of white and pink oleander; behind them, on the right, the arid rocks and harsh vegetation of the mountainous areas; to our left, unseen but imagined, Poodle Rock, where we swim and snorkel and walk through the burnished line of sunset gold into the warmth of sea, as hills deepen into crimson and lilac.

Home, to a newly-created front garden – full of Night Scented Stock and honeysuckle, colours (of beans and butterflies and iridescent turquoise Carpenter Bees) now hidden in the balmy early-morning air, the Moon full and bright.

Fabulous to be back!

Seated at a table, at three/four in the morning, we all drank wine and ate fresh cherries and talk, talk, talked until the adolescent duo were nodding with weariness in their shared home-made turquoise seat.

And now, dozy with raspberry raki, and wine so red it shone, and all the old favourites on the food front, we have returned from our first visit to Vassilis' taverna in Kastellos.

Cicadas rub and roister; many birds sing; butterflies, huge ones, flitter in a stately dance through the tall bean plants.

A furry flurry of odd-shaped dogs under the table, the big white one leaping up the wall in ecstasy whenever she spotted the cat. Cockerels and goats, sharing scrub land, pecking and munching in mid-afternoon heat.

Ah! The wonderful Cretan stories already! Vassilis' dog, who worries sheep and once had a goat by the throat (which sounds like something out of a Dr Seuss book!); an acquaintance, L, whose teenage son sneaked into the family car, letting the handbrake off – and L, busy in the fields, watching in horror as the car, with the youth at the wheel, careered backwards down the family's drive, crossed the (fortunately empty) road and reversed into the wall opposite. No injury – other than to the car!

Through the midday heat haze, and the drowsing hum of vibrant flowers alight with nectar-seeking creatures, I catch a feline drama upon the high stone balcony opposite. The home of Maria...

...elderly and stooped, a white-haired spinster in this land of fecundity, met in the darkness of a steep path late last night, her deep voice, cackling out syllables of irascible Greek, smoothed by the sweetness of wild jasmine...

...and her many cats: six, last night, late-sunning themselves in the dying rays of a magnificent sunset; now, at the point of noon, a shaggy brown moggy copulating with the sultry little queen, both balanced on the thin lip of the outer wall – and watched, dare I say it, by a big caramel-coloured tom, and the weaving beauty of huge scarlet geraniums; instant change over, as one tom gives way to the next, the white, almond-eyed female, not long out of kitten-hood, passive beneath bucking tufts of rampancy, yowls this time, deep and gutteral...

...interrupted, mid-thrust, by Maria's voice calling, 'Merina! Hera!' - and me, in deckchair, sunning pale limbs, uncertain whether 'twas the cats she called or the goddesses of the Olympian line!

And now I see her hobbling, clad in cardigan the same hue as the geraniums, going about her tasks.

A bell tolls. Once. Nasturtiums, trailing their bright orange and lemon flowers down the side of a vast terracotta coloured vase, reach up to the sun.

As do I, in moderation; as do I.

Battling, as ever, the anxiety which locks muscles and births pain, I don the snorkelling mask and struggle out to the clarity of water above dark rocks – and there, star-fished above the underwater scene, I am briefly quiescent, watching three fish going about their lives.

Ah! But such simple things catch me out, don't they? Silly me! Contact lenses and the way they slip and slide, so that the ease for others becomes impossible, and I retreat, replace them with glasses, chide myself: the fear of pain – and the pain of fear – making a peaceful, relaxing swim into a giant war between mind and body.

But, sipping Lemon Verbena, picked fresh from the garden; watching Son, up the orange tree, plucking warm oranges and handing them down to J, I reflect that fighting my own worrisome nature is pointless. I cannot be other than I am. Berating myself for the spiralling terror of aches and pains makes the tension worse. Feeling that I need to prove that I am unafraid, that I can do things the same way as others, is madness glossed with the inviting paint of pseudo-courage.

Now? A brown paper bag full of goodies from the baker, bought by Son and J – one each, we are told. Kind, thoughtful boys. Cheese and chocolate pastries.

The others plunge into the action of life fearlessly. Something I envy. Failing in this regard, I cast my net for word-fish, and attempt, from their glittering scales, to extract the juice of the day, the country, the shining guts of experience.

Down we went last night, to the half-finished kafeneio, and greeted Manolis.

He is having two beautiful stone arches built – by Yiannis, who created Host and Hostess' wonderful wall – and he is afraid that such a labour of love, and money, will not work; that people will continue to flock to a nearby taverna, and that his vision will never be manifest.

But, through the dust, the sheeted tables, the covered kitchen, Ancient Crete is emerging – the arches a bridge between those long-gone times and now, this twenty-first century since the birth of the Christos.

We sat, the six of us, at one of the tables outside – and Manolis brought us hot pork cooked in wine, fresh sardines, slices of cheese, rusks steeped in olive oil and herbs, aubergine dip (creamy and delicious), a hot meat and pepper dish and the dried rusks so common in Armenoi. Gorgeous, though I was so tired, I could barely speak.

This morning, much pain – from my fruitless fight against the spear of fear. Better, by far, to let its painful point enter and lance away the psychic infection, heal the wound, allow me to let go. I felt like a failure, surrounded by people who seemed more normal.

Vassilis arrived, returning a Jeep (which we are to borrow while we are here) – and we sat, the five adults, at the big table in the front garden, talking of bees and their importance, and the skew-whiff nature of the way the world judges quality. Vassilis spoke, with passionate eloquence, of the difference bees make to the true wealth of the world: of the way we crave the pills and potions produced by the great multinational medical conglomerations; how they line the coffers of the greedy pharmaceutical companies; how these would lose out if we were to utilise the natural remedies to be found, free, upon so many trees and bushes.

And then to Biral, the Cretan version of Coca Cola, and squares of fresh melon, the first of the summer – and, later this week, we'll do the Old Town, Rethymno, at night.

Candelabra, built out of wood by Hostess' brother, are centrally placed upon the table outside, cheap white candles dripping fairy tales in wax down their sides and up high.

Food upon the table – and a sudden spasm of stomach pain. Wine ignored – and then, later, stupidly drunk, along with two glasses of apricot-flavoured raki – and a night of horrible pain, abdomen spasming every few seconds for hours and hours. Trying to relax, to remember the meditation moves without the tape, panicking and tensing, making a bad situation worse.

Eventually, I slept – for perhaps two hours – and woke, aching in back and shoulders, but free of the griping abdominal pain.

J. was sick during the night, which makes me wonder if something we ate disagreed with us both.

This morning, bundled into the two jeeps, we drove up the dusty mountain roads, past a dog, tethered by shepherd in a lay-by; past goats and a ewe; past solar panels and the hazy purple-blue of the mountains, up to a breath-taking view over Rethymno – sea and city shining bright in the heat, and Jerusalem sage picked and placed in my handbag.

Back we drove, stopping at the kafeneio, both arches now up, and the wall behind the first being filled in. Looking amazing!

Hilarious malapropism by Son this morning.

'So tell me,' Host asked him, 'what dangers might you find in Nepal?'

'Well,' Son said, seriously, 'those mountain passes are very narrow and I might get charged by an angry yam...'

How I laughed! How I still laugh, thinking about it.

Son's on good form today, and no mistake. They had a huge great hornet, red and yellow, in their room.

'Gather you've got a hornet!' quoth I.

'Well, I don't like to brag...' Son riposted laconically.

Then, on the way down to Poodle Rock:

'That goat's got enormous udders!' (Son)

'Why are you even looking?' (J.)

This evening, we swam at Poodle Rock – while Host fished at the salt mines just up the coast. Harsh drive down – but beautiful, with giant rocks, vivid red earth (like splashes of blood) and the sea just below.

Earlier, on our drive up the mountain, we saw a giants' dance of vultures circling above the sad figure of a moribund sheep.

Rattling back up the track, both Jeeps in use, we were stopped by a great milling brainlessness of sheep and goats, all baaing and bell-tolling and getting in the way.

Sun had slipped down by then, a fragile coin of peachy-gold – and the sky was settling into its sunset blanket of Post-Apocalyptic pastel shades.

Impatient, the boys roared at the hapless ovines and capricorns:

'F*** off!' they bellowed, to helpless guffaws from me – and the flock, sensing authority, or possibly death, in the offing, obediently went forth and multiplied.

Before finding her spouse, Hostess took us up steps cut into the cliff – and, at the top, behind the tiny church of St Nicholas, there was a big cavern, with a naturally 'carved' statue of what looked, to me, like the Goddess – and, as I went closer, looked more like lovers entwined. Pinks and grey and greens gave this figure colour.

In front, there was a hunched figure – again rock formation grown over the millions of years the cave has existed.

There was even a small grave pit in the north.

'Perfect for ritual,' I thought to myself.

The sea, yesterday, warmed quickly and was a delight to swim and float and laze in.

Today – and up early – we four adults went into Rethymno to visit the Thursday market.

183

Having got through the streams of irritable Cretans honking horns, and shouting at one another, we parked at the Marina. All was beautiful outside, though very hot.

The market was crammed with fresh fruit and vegetables: cherries, aubergines, oranges, lemons, onions, garlic, courgettes – stall after stall of luscious colours and tempting aromas. We found yogurt and honey, herbs, eggs, olives and the huge doughnuts we have bought in previous years.

On the way back, we stopped at a kafeneio. It was lovely and cool, in a shady niche between two sweltering roads. Beer, Coke and a plate of rusks, cheese and olives revived us – and it was then back home, to find the lads up and doing, Son in a superb teal-coloured Cretan shirt.

On the way home from Rethymno, we had consumed great handfuls of the ripe cherries, as the heated air blew my hair every which way.

The cherries, so greedily gorged, were a mistake. That and the ever-present anxiety, and the thought of slathering up for the drive to Souda Bay. Sudden epigastric pain – second time in two days – assailed me. The physical response to anticipated stress was immediate, terrifying and saddening.

I lay down on the bed for ten minutes or so, and relaxed: the pain lifted.

The drive, along the mountain roads, through the Kotsifou Canyon, and down towards Souda, was sublime. Such beauty, with the greenery, the flowers, the ever-present smells of thyme and sage; the bright blues, teals and turquoise shades of the Mediterranean; the starkness of rock; the high vaulting mountains themselves – and that delightful heat, enjoyed through wide-open windows.

At the little beach just before Souda, the sea was rough, a churning, though warm, mess of detritus. Snorkelling was not possible, and poor Husband got sun cream in his eye and was in considerable pain.

Souda was exquisite – and a revelation for me: I can do things! A wide expanse of beach, cliffs to the right and loads of wonderful blue sea to play in.

In we went. Minutes later, I donned Host's prescription snorkelling mask and, with almost no hesitation, dove into the underwater world. It was lovely watching the fish as they went about their busy little lives: magical and such a confidence boost.

After a warm shower on the beach, I lay on a towel on the sand – and just let the sun sink into my pale body and troubled mind. That, in itself, was healing, and I thought, 'If I did this once a week, my stress levels would soon come down!'

We drove back as the sun began to wane, and stopped at a taverna. Lovely place – delightful people and delicious food; cheap too – thirty-five Euros for a large meal, for all six of us!

As we sat and ate, and drank two carafes of pale golden retsina, the sun began its glorious descent, painting the ridges of the White Mountains a wonderful rose colour – utterly breath-taking and oddly moving.

Meandering back home, looking at the great expanses of contrasting aridity and flowering abundance, the mountains and the flatter lands, the curves, the gorse bushes, the dying shades of pinky-mauve still draping the hills' shoulders, we met an old man, walking along the road, a man known to our hosts.

Gentle greetings; hands clasped through open windows; gossip exchanged.

Later, I wrote a piece about Rethymno — and the friend I sent an email copy to thought it excellent. I have trimmed its more vituperative sails in order for it to float out into the big wide world — but, I confess I am pleased with it, and feel that it is approaching the pared-back, sensual style I am making my own.

I tend, these days, to plunge in, bucking like a wild horse — or, to continue the oceanic imagery, undulating like a dolphin! - and grab the herbs, the colours, the sensations which make up the broth from which atmosphere is ladled. Narrative conformity is not my forte.

No need to be afraid or apologetic. There are countless other writers who do tell a tale with verve and energy; we do not all have to be the same.

Tonight we will return to the Old Town, Rethymno, and go to Goran's taverna to eat. This will be lovely.

I am reading Victoria Hislop's 'The Island', a wonderful, if sad, book about Crete – specifically about the Leper Colony on the island of Spinalonga, and the way it was abandoned in the late fifties, after a cure for leprosy was found.

Yesterday, I visited the Bakery. It is much changed. They no longer have a little dog to terrify the traffic and risk its own life every hour of the day. But they did have a most tempting array of pastries and ice creams and other delicacies.

Later: giant sun, a tracing of thinnest gold through the mid-evening sky, a wedding band from Day to Night – hand-fasting of the twenty-four hours! Down into Rethymno, along the sea front, huge concrete jacks ready to tumble onto the harbour's checker-board; young people, two to a motorbike, shirt sleeves, no helmets, happy, relaxed; the air, scented, strongly at times, with thyme, Crete's olfactory signature tune; neon 'eyes' winking purple, blue, green, red, gold; my body stiff with over-heated irritation (temperature 28 degrees at 9pm); striding ahead in long, green-patterned Indian dress, caught between youth and middle age, I wanted to run and cry and scream and laugh, and have fun, be spontaneous – Oh! The weight of adulthood upon my reluctant bones and wild spirit.

Lowest tide; dinosaur bones of rock straddling the sea's bed; the Fortezza arrow-slitting us back into the invasions we all inherit and ignore at our peril; modern day Pirate Ship Jack Sparrowing its way across the bay, tilting its cutlass at the Cretan sun.

And so to Goran's taverna, and a table for six, right at the cool end, adjacent to the alley full of undulating, yowling cats.

Food shared, while the beggars came calling, with their tacky wares and stegosaurus hides: a tall young woman with her sack full of glitter-strewn Disney monstrosities, and her little sister, garish in green and ghastly upon the accordion – both ignored.

Serbian delicacies – Alvar, the delectable red pepper dip; the richness of tiny meatballs; octopus; jazzed-up potatoes; organic red wine.

Then, suddenly, a rough diamond in the great jewellers' shop of artifice, there was, a tiny boy, seven or so, dark of complexion and hair, trying to coax 'Never on a Sunday' out of the recalcitrant crimson and white keys of the accordion he had slung round his neck.

But his voice, when he sang, was deep and true – mesmerising in this irritating wee scrap of humanity who, waiflike, insinuated himself closer and closer to the people at each table, singing little snatches of song and crying, quite blatantly, 'Money! Money!'

Goran, using his arms as a gentle broom, tried to brush the little urchin away – but he would not go. Our laughter revitalised him, and he mugged for the invisible camera, until he was shooed inside and told to find the kitchen and the warm goodies therein.

Off he went, then, down Cat Alley, still singing, still cheeky and insouciant, and somehow brave and rather sweet. Such spirit and determination; such boldness; I couldn't help warming to him.

We wandered back, seeing a young lady, pliant as a pipe cleaner, clad in harem pants and a scanty top, juggling two torches; we stopped for ice cream – and, oh, the succulent softness of the flavours on offer left me entranced. I wanted all of them – the smooth mauve, the tempting toffee, laid-back coffee, rich and deep chocolate!

In the end, chocolate won. Cone clutched in left hand, I licked and luxuriated – and, in the 25 degree heat of midnight, allowed great splashes of melt to bleed into hands and chin and dress – until, back on the promenade, I wandered, gazing at the darkness of sea, and the lights of all the tavernas and shops still open.

We found the two Jeeps – and, windows wide open, drove back home, a cooling breeze lifting the orange strands of hair off my hot face and damp neck.

That, my dears, is the essence of Rethymno Old Town at night!

New day dawned – and it appeared deceptively cool as we set off, at midday, for the South Coast.

The winding mountainous drive was spectacular: scrub land, olive trees, bright orange geraniums, pink, white and peach oleander, and always the harsh unrelenting beauty of Cretan rock, in places pale green.

At one point, high up, we stopped – and, easing ourselves from the hot leather of car seats, walked up the mountain road, seeing great purple 'mushrooms' of wild thyme bushes; seeing the black and brown mountain goats, with their huge bells clonging and clanging; picking, in my case, spiky handfuls of the fragrant natural scent of this land, and pushing them down into a side pouch of my handbag, there to mingle with lavender and Jerusalem sage.

Quite suddenly, we came across an old, rusted and broken-down van, painted, with startling and humorous colour, by WD, the Cretan Banksy: Alice in Wonderland, cup held in left hand, smiled mysteriously from the front panel; whilst the Cheshire Cat (anything but mysterious; downright sinister, I would have said!) leered, smirked and gurned (think mating between feline and shark!) from the foetid inner recesses of said auto-mobile; the White Rabbit, fetchingly etched on the far right, gave every appearance of being about to scurry off the van altogether.

As we gazed and mused, a car stopped and a dark-complexioned youth stepped out, and began to saunter van-wards.

'Ah! The Banksy himself!' someone exclaimed.

We pointed. He smiled.

'You painted that?' one of us asked.

'Is very good,' he said, and then shook his head and smiled, pointing to the small herd of goats tolling their way up the road. 'My goats!'

'Lovely!' I said, torn between that and, 'Well done, that man!'

So there he was, a humble goatherd, dropped off by twenty-first century conveyance, modern technology (ipod) stuck in his ears, clambering up the hillside to do the job done by peasants right back through history to Ancient Crete.

Next was Triopetra Beach, a long stretch bound, on the left hand side, by the three rocks which gave it its name. Quite a flurry of excitement - and on the boys' part, thinly-disguised disgust! - when we saw a few nudists pottering about. Mostly middle-aged and, frankly, past their best, they turned our heads, and the teens' stomachs, with equal force.

Jokingly, I said, 'Well, I'd be quite happy to whip my kit off and go nude!'

Son groaned.

'I'm disowning you if you do, Mum,' he said. 'Need at least three beaches between us if you even think of it!'

Hmmm!

Can't say I blame him, though: I would have been equally horrified, in my teens, had my old dear shown even the remotest signs of traipsing across Budleigh Salterton beach sky-clad.

Then the beach, with its central enclave of sun-loungers, matching parasols and skimpily-clad Baby Boomers wearing inadequate cotton wisps against leathery naked skin, upped the ante on the under twenties' revolted horror hugely. To my relief, there was a taverna – well, kind of: a driftwood shack, vaguely boat-shaped, with a few tables and a most welcoming and friendly young man.

In we went – and, over glasses of Fix, and oregano-flavoured crisps (dipped in Mayonnaise – yum!), we people-watched and made desultory conversation.

I went for a walk along the beach. The sand was incredibly hot – but, fortunately, a walkway, created by planks of wood, had been laid in a haphazard line.

Shells there were none, but I found some beautiful pebbles, green, red, pink and yellowy-gold, picked them, warm and wet and salt-smelling, from the sea's tongue and clutched them in my left hand.

On we drove, to the delightful beach at Agios Pavlos – and swam and snorkelled for ages. I saw several brightly-coloured parrot fish, one with a blue head and green body.

Yesterday, we drove to the Aradhena Gorge. Stark scrub-land, scorching day; clouds like beaten egg-white against an impossibly-blue sky – and, peering down, the mysterious cleft of the gorge, a giant vagina cut into the land's body. It was so hot that I could not, initially, bear to leave the car – and watched, in torpid silence, as the others clambered over rocks and took photos.

Over the rickety bridge we drove, its planks rattling loudly. I did not look down – partly fear and partly a wish to keep the gorge's secrets a little longer.

Slathering up with factor sixty, I followed the others through a gate into the rocky landscape of the abandoned village. Giant molars of stone lay broken all around – decayed teeth in the dead mouth of a previously-thriving community, its denizens driven out by feud and vendetta, this being the very heart of Bandit Country.

The small graveyard had recent dead buried in it, despite the fact that the village was deserted some thirty years ago. People born there returned to their roots, which I found oddly touching.

Red soil and small spiny bushes; loose stones and tiny purple flowers; an abandoned church, still full of Greek Orthodox finery.

The path twisted down, down, down, hard on knee and thigh; fear of slipping, of twisting an ankle, kept me slow and hesitant at first – but, by the time we reached the bottom, I was gathering pace and confidence.

The gorge itself was stunning: great red cliffs soared up; there was a real sense of otherworldliness: Tolkienesque; full of the mystery of ritual and ancient gods and ancient peoples; giant rocks, a wide path; the bridge seen from the bottom; goats, bones of dead animals, fissures and caves.

I wanted to close my eyes – and just feel the past embracing me and my present self. I had a strong sense of priests and priestesses winding their way along such places, on their way to celebrate an important festival, a Full Moon, a birth, a death, a visit to the Oracle.

Returning from this deep and ancient wound in the earth, we climbed. The sun was fierce, the going hard – very hard; I began to falter, to panic, to over-breathe; I feared I would not reach the top in one piece.

But I did it! Red of face, breathing harshly, near tears and feeling nauseous, I pushed myself on until I reached the summit – and, for a few minutes, sat under the relative shelter of a tree, for the sun was still a force to be reckoned with at five in the afternoon.

I recovered quickly – and began to feel light of heart, and so relieved that I had not given up half way.

The final scrabble up a shallow bank of spiky, scratchy vegetation was almost joyous, though the heat rays still raked all exposed skin, and sent rivers of sweat down the craters between body and clothing.

Thirty years ago, before the bridge was built, the only way the villagers could get in and out of their village was the long and arduous walk we had just done. Incredible, when you think about it: black-clad grannies toiling their way along these ancient and hazardous paths day after day!

The bridge brought fear. The planks of wood had gaps. I made sure I did not look down, knowing that I would be assailed by vertigo if I did. I rushed over, trying not to give way to the primal fear that I would slip between the cracks – which, in the nature of these things, seemed to widen ever further the more I looked at them.

But, oh the sense of achievement when I reached the other side – and, leaning over the stone wall, saw how deep we'd gone and how far we had climbed.

A final meal at Castello taverna marked the end of our lovely holiday.

The plane journey home was full of incident, shall we say. Oh! The humiliation! On the outward-bound flight, the metal fiddly bits in my ruby-coloured slippers set the alarm off, and I had to be patted down by one of Bristol Airport's finest.

So, to be on the safe side, I dressed very carefully in a long dress, espadrilles and underwear for the Trial by Chania Airport – a breeze, I was quite sure.

Wrong!

The other three – all weighed down with watches, belts, metallic widgets and God only knows what else – sailed through Security. By ghastly contrast, as soon as I went under the Doorway of Doom, bells started ringing, lights flashed, klaxons wailed – and about fifteen security guards approached me.

I was told to stand still. A few other people trickled through, craning their necks to stare at me. Then a squat bulldog of a woman muscled up to me – and pushed me into a cubical. She was wearing protective gloves!

She had a wand/scanner thing which she waved over my body. It beeped like hell. The Cretan Mastiff frowned; actually, she may have growled and bared a few teeth.

Without so much as a 'By your leave,' she had that wand up my skirt, and heading in the direction of my intimate crevices, shall we say? What the bloody hell she hoped/expected to find up there I have no idea – and was in no mood to ask either.

Finally, after a couple of years had passed, she announced that the villain of the piece had been my bra. Ye gods! This is getting ridiculous! Do I have to go through Security bosom-naked in future?

Still – had I been a suicide bomber, intent upon blowing us all into the next life courtesy of a double E cup stuffed with Semtex, that guard would have had me banged to rights and no mistake.

Even if her wand-waving was, initially, a tad off-piste.

On the other hand, no terrorist with half a brain cell is going to attract as much attention as I, inadvertently, did – and, on both occasions, whilst my shoes and tit-holsters were being examined, hordes of clever buggers – with noxious substances stashed in orifices large and small – would, no doubt, be smiling smugly, and looking as if butter wouldn't melt in their cake holes!

PART FOUR

Monday 27th July – Monday 10th August 2015

Tuesday 28th July

It is late morning – and sitting at a table on the balcony outside my room, I feel happy, free in a very real sense. Part of this is the fact that I seem to be zooming through the tunnels of fear, and out the other side, with ever-increasing speed.

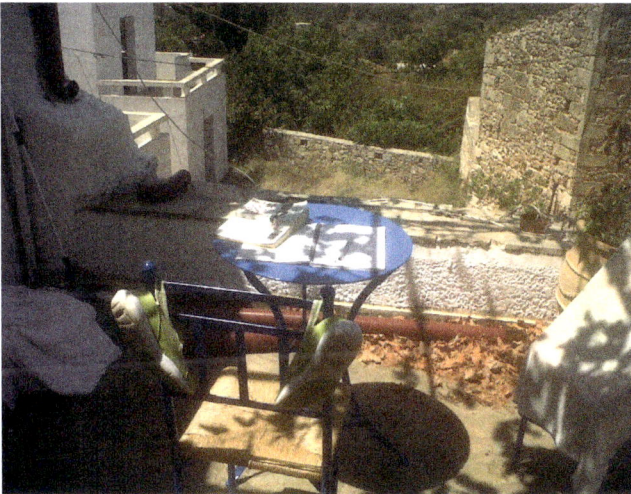

Another aspect revolves around Son having his girlfriend, A, with him this year. But the main reason (however selfish this may seem) is the sense I have of becoming me once again, the Alienora I should be.

And of course, this is such a beautiful and special place, for a landscape writer like myself, that I leap in joy and revel in the senses so generously at my disposal.

It is, if you like (and personally I do!), the upside of my physical barometer – and two weeks of my body responding with increasing immediacy to life's pleasures can only have a positive effect upon a frazzled mind.

It is very hot – in the thirties, at a guess. The mountains shimmer, and hide demurely in a liberty bodice of heat. Cicadas shiver limbs together in an ecstasy of lust.

Rains (unusual at this time of year) have left the island unusually luscious, leaves bright green, with big flowers, in shades of pink, orangey-peach and white, lining the roadsides.

The vines, trellised above my head out here, are withered-looking, their leaves falling in great swathes, almost as if it were autumn as opposed to summer and four days before the Lughnasad Full Moon. The month to come has two full moons, one of which will be a Blue Moon.

The sky is a seamless, cloudless bowl of heat. The tiny grapes are hard, green. The grape harvest has, once again, been ruined – and, in this land of financial hardship, this will bite hard. The Germans, in tightening the Iron Maiden of tax, are poised to bring Crete to its knees. It is so sad, so unnecessary – cruelty and greed ruling common sense and compassion.

Vassilis waxed passionate about the whole situation last night, after a lovely meal, and an astonishing event/encounter.

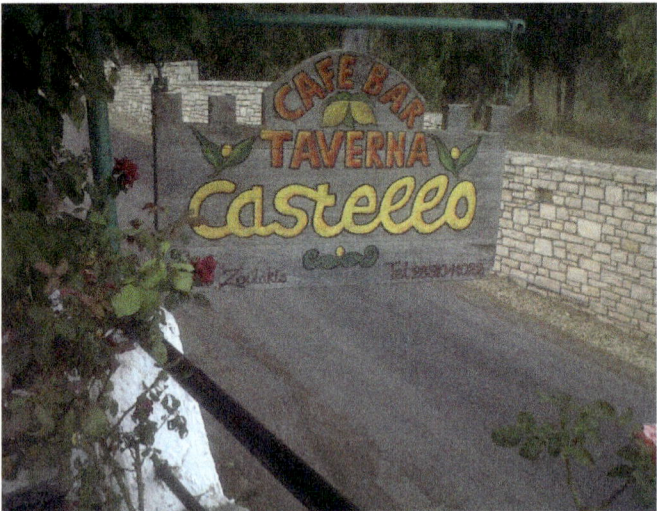

The six of us sat at the table nearest Castello Taverna's bar – and, looking around I saw a family of six (French, as it transpired) at the next table: mother, father and four little girls (including twins).

Using mostly body language, and a few words of French, I befriended two of the girls – and, as I communed with the children, I heard the Maman say what sounded like, 'Alienor...' to the tiniest of the offspring – and, unable to believe the evidence of my own ears, went over and asked if I had heard correctly.

To my utter delight, I *had*: the sweet blonde three year old had been named (as I was) after Eleanor/Alienor of Aquitaine.

'I am Alienora!' I told the parents.

They looked as thrilled and amazed as I felt: little Alienor had never met anyone else with her name, nor, until that moment in a Cretan taverna, had I.

The mother (whose English was very good) told Yiannis (whose home they are renting) and we all beamed excitedly at one another.

Just amazing, though: fifty-seven (and a half, to be precise!) years of thinking myself the only Alienora – and, by complete happenchance, I bump into my infant namesake (well, near as can be: what's an 'a' between friends?), in a Cretan taverna way off the tourist track.

What are the chances of that, eh?

I came back to our table so excited, told the others.

Later: Ah! Very hot still. I have been siesta-ing (is that actually a word? If not, it jolly well should be!) for a couple of hours, and am now back on the balcony. It's almost too bright for comfort, and a nearby frenzy of cicadas are making a hell of a racket, punctuated by a brief (and presumably shagged-out!) silence.

The journey/flight out here was a revelation and a pleasure, though the sky looked unpromising in the extreme when A's parent called for us at four in the morning: cold, cloud-strewn sky, rain pouring down, about as grey and depressing as it is possible to imagine.

Though very tired (having only slept for about two hours), I was excited rather than terrified. This made me think about adrenaline in terms of a pair of scales, with fear on one side and excitement on the other – but still essentially the same instrument.

This led me to wonder just how important it actually is to live in absolute balance, with both sides equally weighted – and wonder if there might not be a case made for balance becoming stasis, and even satiation/ennui, in some people. Those who need constant stimulation from external sources may be low on natural adrenaline.

I don't know! I am not a scientist. It's just a thought.

Be that as it may: we suddenly realised (thanks to Son) that the boarding gate for our Ryanair flight was closing in five minutes – so we hot-footed it up stairs, along corridors dotted with the scattered detritus of other late Chania-bound mortals – and joined the Priority queue (thanks to Husband), and were on the plane by about 6.20 am.

There was an unspecified, in terms of length, delay (due to Traffic Control problems the other end) which meant that we didn't actually take off until nearly seven.

A hilarious little sign seen in the ladies loo: an intimate aid (shall we say!), entitled,

'Play: Stimulation Ring For Both Sexes,' which made me both squirm in discomfort (the mechanics of it sounding truly ghastly!) and howl with ribald laughter, rude moo that I am.

Oh! That moment, when the big plane turned right on the runway, and its stately taxiing turned into turbo-boost's full-throttled roar, was fabulous. I love the anticipation and excitement of it all, especially the bit when the plane's nose lifts (in Patrician disdain at the British weather, I like to think!) - and we're off, up into the skies.

We climbed steeply this time, to the accompaniment of the usual light-headed feeling and temporary deafness, arriving in the Land of White Meringue Clouds. They appeared so soft and lovely that I was quite enchanted.

And, as we rose above them, I realised something amazing: that, irrespective of the weather, the sky above the clouds is blue! That really touched me for some reason. It just seemed to say something wonderful about our brave and beautiful Earth – and, by extension, since we are intimately connected, about the human spirit. I guess the metaphor goes like this: no matter how dark the skies, somewhere, high above, there is beautiful blue and sun.

There was minor turbulence – but I remained so calm that I simply carried on reading 'The Priestess of Avalon'.

At around ten, we began the descent, and I felt tearful when I saw the craggy landscape of Crete, and what looked like every single wave in the sunlit turquoise of the sea.

It is now about 8.15 pm, and cooling down at last, my memories of the flight disappearing like mist. The artists are coming over for sundown – and then we are all going to a taverna down the road, to see a lyra player (and his band, one assumes!), and steep ourselves in Cretan music and dancing.

I felt no fear as we drove from Chania to Armenoi. This, in itself, is interesting – and a good sign, I feel.

The evening outline of the mountains, as the sun begins to set, is endlessly fascinating, beautiful and moving to me: such lucidity of shape, such stunning richness of colour - from, the golds and rose-golds as the sun tucks itself behind ancient rock, to the pinks, crimsons and purples of the afterglow. The latter is especially lovely when traced, cut and embroidered over the darkening blue bodice of the sea, the two biggest peaks at the Western edge of Poodle Rock looking like breasts cupped in the deep mauve of a titanic brassiere.

Wednesday 29th July

A combination of too much sun and beer has given me a slightly upset stomach this morning.

It is 10.30 am, and there is a haziness in the air, a slight thermal muffling of the mountains that betokens temperatures in the mid-thirties later. A breeze softens things, but I would be wise not to stay on the balcony for too long, sheltered though it is.

Thursday 30th July

Hot morning already – and it is only about 10.15.

We have been to the Rethymno market. The colourful underwear section always makes me laugh, especially the gallimaufry of bras, in every shade of the rainbow, and catering to all sizes from pre-teen to ones suitable for Eccentrica Gallumbits, the triple breasted whore of Eroticon 6.

Lingerie gawped at, we stopped at the little courtyard taverna just over the road for drinks, and the tender fluttering of turtle doves.

Secreted in a trellis of vibrantly-pink bougainvillea, the small family of doves seemed so young and shyly sweet that I found myself touched by their antics. At

one point, there was a fluttering of youthful wings indicative of joyous mating; prior to that, it appeared as if they were making the food stop at Mama Dove's kitchen. Bless!

The market was, as ever, a riot of colour: vibrant reds, oranges and greens jostling for attention with the subtler hues of creamy cheese and the variegated natural tones of honey.

The sea looked exquisite – a shimmering expanse of turquoise, sparkling in a sun already in excess of any heat one gets in the UK.

The Fortezza was bathed in honey-gold magnificence.

Back on the Balcony outside my room – and I am looking at the pinky-white smear of the White Mountains, and listening to the usual orchestra of bonking insects: delightful.

After our evening swim at Poodle Rock, we retired to the terrace taverna above (Babis) and tucked into fresh food, while watching the sun go down.

Monday, we went in convoy to the lovely beach at Polyrizos – had a light lunch in the beachside taverna and then dove into the warm clarity of sea.

For complicated reasons (which I won't go into: life's too short!), I couldn't get a snorkelling mask to work for me – but, in a very real sense, this did not matter. The water was so pellucid that I could see the little fish (tiny mullet, silvery anchovies and a small flatfish) as they darted between rocks or, in the case of the mullet, formation-glided on the surface of the water.

The journey, punctuated by stops to pick herbs, was fun. We were travelling at a stately pace, which meant that we were able to enjoy the minutiae of the landscape – and there was much chat, banter and laughter between the four of us.

Monday evening moved seamlessly into Tuesday morning - and we drove down the road a tad, turning left in order to revisit both the Minoan Cemetery and Vangelis' wonderfully wide-ranging museum in Somatas.

In the effort-laden heaviness of heat, we walked round those ancient graves, descending the steps of the biggest – and walking into the pale-green and white-walled shock of cool air, and slugs clamped into rough question marks upon the old stone; a crescendo of crickets in musical notation upon the ceiling – and the sense of there having been an important personage interred there once upon a very long time ago.

The visit to the Somatas Museum was very emotional. The photo of Son and Vangelis (taken way back in 2010, and a print given to the old man in 2011) had pride of place on the beams of the outer, barn-type, room – and when Vangelis made the connection, he beamed broadly and put his arm around Son.

We got the guided tour and a glass of raki each. Much laughter and many photos later, Vangelis gave us a green bottle of home-made raki, and off we went.

Post Somatas, we went to the kafeneio in Armenoi and, having ordered drinks, asked if Manolis could rustle up some food for us. This he did, bless him – bringing courgette omelette, fish, salad, rusks and rice-stuffed courgette leaves. Delicious. Son was brilliant — such ease with others, and becoming ever-more confident and assertive in this kind of situation. I felt so proud of him.

The Moon, waxing, was glorious. It had moved from Sunday's perky maiden breast, pink as the blush of first sexual awakening, to something fuller and more mature/experienced.

The artists arrived — and the eight of us sat in the front garden, and ate pistachios and drank retsina before setting off in two vehicles for the lyra event in Pale (a village about ten minutes' drive from Armenoi).

The sky opened out into a muted deep pink — and, as soon as sun set and light faded, the cicadas redoubled their racket, as if something in the softly-encroaching darkness were an erotic switch.

Yes, we drove to Pale (pronounced 'Pa-lay') through the ghostliness of grey mountains under a darkening sky, a beautiful drive as I discovered when we went that way again today.

The lyra player was great, as was the left-handed bouzouki player; the band also had a guitarist and a drummer.

The French family, first met in Castello Taverna, also came – and joined our table. My little namesake wanted to touch me (as if wondering if I were actually real!), which I thought very sweet. My evening was punctuated by little starfish hands clutching me gently (touching in every sense)

The dancing was patchy and somewhat restrained – a shame because I wanted to just get up there and go wild!

I am happy, my skin becoming a pale gold in colour. I ration the pleasure of visits to the balcony's heat, taking a few moments here and there – but feeling the need of the sun, both sensually and poetically. Puts me in mind of the D.H Lawrence short story all about the white, English girl, Juliet, receiving the attentions of the sun as one would a lover – first read that Pembrokeshire Coast Path summer (1977), in the musky pre-dawning of my full sexual awakening, and connected now, in sensual intensity, to the ancient brightness of Crete.

This landscape and its people, its food and wine and animals and way of life combine to awaken something dormant in me as a writer.

Yesterday, we set off along the mountain roads (past Iphigenia's on the way out, and through the Kotsifou Canyon on the way back), in glorious heat and at a sedate pace, cloudless skies shading into the olive and green magnificence of mountains.

We parked just up from a most wonderful and weird museum, tucked away deep in the winding white-washed alleyways of the village of Asomatas. Mountains encircled us, their bony flanks stark against the midday heat – and the intense sparkling blue of South Coast beaches.

The museum, whitewashed and decorated with reds and greens, consisted of the lifetime's collection made by an obsessive hoarder. It was disturbing, macabre (Chucky-type dolls, all his daughter's shoes from birth to eighteen etc) – and, in places, lovely.

The collector, Papa Michaelis, was a priest who died in 2008. His son, a lovely guy around my age (at a guess), now owns the collection and runs the museum (a series of rooms opening from a central, and very pretty, courtyard).

Several brightly-coloured Greek Orthodox robes hung in glass cabinets.

'Vestments' is, perhaps, a more accurate word in terms of religious vocabulary; but 'robes' to me conjures up a central tenet of spiritual truth: all gods are one god; all goddesses, one goddess.

Papa Michos was evidently, and understandably, a difficult man to live with – and I believe his wife, son(s) and daughter decamped from the family abode.

The son (like Vassilis) felt very strongly about the German 'offer' and its effective stranglehold over Greece – and the suspicion that Germany is going to attempt to annexe smaller nations, using financial 'aggression', the way it did with military might in the thirties and forties.

He (the son) felt that Greece should come out of the European Union, reject the Euro, bring back the Drachma.

We sat in a lovely, narrow offshoot of the courtyard, and drank coffee, then visited the ceramics shops, sampling their delicious olives and fresh bread dipped in olive oil. I bought eight little beads, each a different colour and bearing one of my name's letters. Mounted on a purple band, they make a lovely, and very unusual, bracelet.

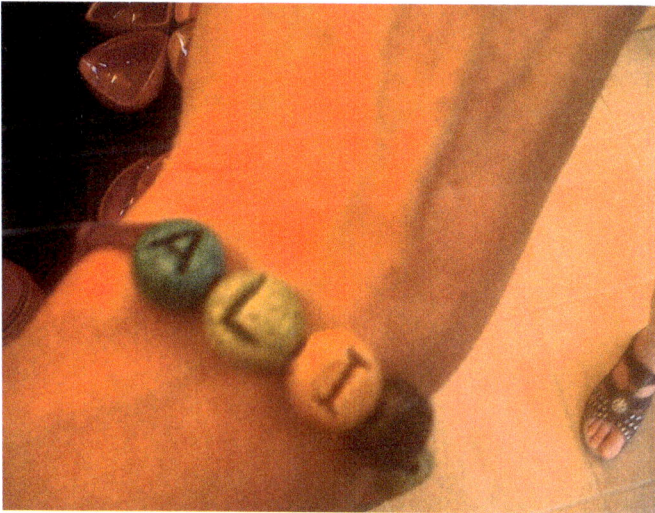

I bought ice creams for everyone – and then we set off, through Plakias, to Souda beach. The sea was gorgeously warm, and I had a short snorkel. Unfortunately, the mask was leaking and I couldn't stay down for long. Everything was so lovely, though, that it was enough just to laze in the sea.

Friday July 31st

A sweaty and breathless night – reminding me that I have not fully acclimatised to the extreme heat as yet, and also bringing me the closest to panic I've had on this holiday so far.

I am out on the balcony. It is 11am, and not too hot to be bearable as yet. As I intimated yesterday, I think it very good for me to open my pale body to the sun, in moderation – and I think I am getting better at judging how long it is safe for me to be out here at any one time.

We ended up at Vassilis' last night – and it was a delight, easily the most equitable, fun meal we have shared thus far: delectable pork with vegetables and cheese; kolokythokeftedes, with pepper (possibly the best I have ever tasted) – and the jugs of Vassilis' red and white wine, so fragrant and subtly, sweetly flavoured; so unlike the hob-nailed boot effect of wines containing preservatives, that, truly, it was like sipping ambrosia and nectar.

We lingered over Chamomile tea and honey when we got back here, and didn't get to bed until gone two as a result.

There is a vague plan to go into Rethymno tomorrow – and take a three hour trip on the Barbarossa (the Pirate Ship) today. I think a lot is going to depend on how hot it gets, because shelter is not guaranteed: 37 degrees today, and feeling 49 degrees! Our hottest day thus far. Definitely not a day to be out and about.

Saturday 1st August

A very welcome breeze, though mountains are heat-hazed already, as if shawled in an ill-fitting invisibility cloak.

Yesterday, we went swimming at Poodle Rock – and the sea was glorious, so warm and supportive that I just lay on my back upon the surface and felt as if I were being rocked in a vast and watery cradle. The sand was uncomfortably hot underfoot – like dipping my toes into the ashy deposit from an erupting volcano. Borderline painful and unpleasant.

There was a small earthquake here yesterday. I was sitting out on the balcony, on one of the chairs, when suddenly there was a lurch, as if someone were pushing me from behind; it was a round, hot and furry sensation, oddly enough. I wasn't frightened so much as startled.

In the evening, we drove north along the Atlantic Road, and out to the village of

Asteri – and the taverna we visited with John, Sofia, Martin and Maria two or three years ago.

Nectario (the dancer from Armenoi) has joined a troupe of traditional Cretan dancers, and last night was his second professional gig. There were six dancers all told, three men and three women – and there was also a band (lyra player, who also sang; keyboard player who doubled on the drums and two guys playing the louta, the Cretan version of the lute).

It was lovely! Fabulous music, excellent dancing (with the chance to join in, which Husband, Son, A and I took several times!)- and a really buzzy, electric atmosphere.

Hostess, Sofia and I went over to Dimitri, the lyra player, and requested 'Olos O Kosmos', and another piece dear to Sofia's heart.

I danced, clapped, called out, whooped, was full of fizz and joy and, yes, spirit.

My sense of aliveness has returned!

But the other thing is this: my light and joy had nothing to do with any human being; it related to the music, the dancing, the constant beauty and inspiration of landscape and heat and Full Moon – and something within myself, cowering for so long, bursting down the doors of fear and emerging, bathed in milky-silver moonlight.

Sunday 2nd August

We have been here a week! In fact, one week ago (it is, at a guess, 7.45 UK time), we were up above the clouds, Crete bound.

This morning, the intense blue of the sky is made mannerly by kerchiefs of cloud, and there is a most welcome wind waving the plants and cooling things down.

The mountains are shadowed, tatterdemalion garments wrought of stitched sun and cloud-shade, their usual sharp outlines dulled. The clouds even contain grey tones – and, indeed, in Rethymno last night, heat cloying and close as unwanted intimacy, the promise of after-sun's cooling tapestry suddenly gave way to an ominous deep grey-blue – and, gasping beneath the trapped heat, I felt two or three large raindrops. For a brief moment, I longed for the sky to crack and boom and zizz with a full-on storm, catching the 98%-rounded taut drum of a waning moon, and easing the pressure.

I was, at the time, in the Old Town's ceramics shop, buying a bracelet of colourful letters for a friend – and the shop's owner caught the raindrops on his fingers, at which point we both looked up at the straining membrane of labouring sky and waited, heads briefly craned, for its waters to break, and the full embryonic form of tempest to bulge from its emptying womb. But, as the guy adjusted the bracelet's blue band, the sky's contractions stopped as suddenly as they had started – and we were left underneath heat's intense waiting game.

The Old Town was lovely: bustling with colour; percussive with the sounds of the human voice drum; bright shops open for us to investigate.

Waves were breaking off into little muscular bunches – and menacing the rocks beneath a dark blue, almost black, sky, broken only by the flawed circle of the waning moon. By contrast, the Fortezza's honey-stone, opposite a classically Homeric wine-dark sea, was lit up as if by a thousand torches – and Rethymno's multi-coloured neon lights blinked and flared, garish as an Acid trip.

I have changed. I can feel that. Since last year, I mean. I am more open, more relaxed, less fearful. I don't feel the need to wear long trousers just in case any more; I flow out and into the sun whenever I can – and my skin is soaking up the rays greedily, turning from pallid milk to softest caramel. I wear my beloved colourful tops, earrings to match, batwing blouses over long black skirt in the evenings, and feel something of my old self returning.

Wednesday 5th August

Early and claggy, but beautiful. Last night's moonrise was extraordinary: a goddess, full-breasted, and her trickled-gold-upon-silvery-milk moment of dipping, with such charm and sensuality, into the sheerest lace of an orange-gold bosom covering, which allowed some semblance of lunar modesty. That pendulous shape, however, that globe of suckling, nurturing motherliness, spoke clear as a Cretan night sky of womanhood and the female mysteries and the deep blood-beat of the landscape, and our connections.

This was augmented by a huge shooting star (red-tinted, spear-shaped: an omen?) - the god-seed ejaculating up into the womb of the firmament.

Ah! I was tired, terse, inclined to be crotchety: eight kilometre walk, with Son and A, down the stunning Imbros Gorge, but the last half hour in decreasing shelter/increasing heat.

The under-twenties found a sun-bleached skull (sheep? Goat?) and posed merrily with it, as I snapped photos and struggled to keep up!

Scene-setting: sitting on the balcony, I survey the waning moon, still a symbol of bosomly abundance, but now shrivelling down to the Crone Phase. How the Moon's cycles mirror those of womanhood!

Still and all, I am proud of myself (a year ago, I wouldn't have attempted such a marathon!) - and delighted in both the landscape and the company of the Young Things!

The six of us drove to the infamous Holly Five Virgins' walk – and while Husband and Host holed up in Lappa, the four of us walked down the rough steps, to the little caves, the graves, the two thousand year old tree and the stone Spring of Eternal Youth – and then meandered back through the mugginess, with me feeling vaguely cranky and out-of-sorts.

The sheer magnificence, and stupefying age, of Lappa gets to me every time: the evidence of Roman habitation; the breath-taking views; the astonishing vibrancy, and colour range, of the many flowers; the white marble top of a baby's sarcophagus (surely pre-dating Christianity), guarding the entrance to a Greek Orthodox church – and then, at the bottom, the Greek/German lady (met several times now) from whom we bought olive oil, oregano and honey raki.

Oh! And then down into the plashing waters and fecund colouration of Argyroupolis – and great hunks of meat which 'breathed' in the fragrant heat of the revolving spit from bloodied and sundered rib-cages.

Barely had we sat down than Son commented that a rat was on the stone floor feet from our table. Determined to face another fear, I was up in a bound, and bore witness to the pathetic little specimen before us: its back legs were useless, curled like vulnerable small pink shrimps; it was dragging them behind it, long tail out flat, barely able to move. Son wanted to pick it up, take it to a place of safety, though I think it was clear to all of us that it was sorely injured and probably in extremis.

The waitress appeared quite suddenly, with a long broom, a dustpan and, later, a bucket. She seemed to be both chivvying, and trying to squash/crush, the wounded creature with the broom. We heard high-pitched squeaking, and then the rat fell onto the ground some feet below – and, following speedily, the woman continued her poking or crushing or whatever it was, the ghastly squealing a Greek chorus to an everyday tragedy.

It stopped in the end, the piteous noise and that small life – and the woman marched off, bucket in one hand, broom in the other.

I know all the reasonable arguments (the vermin/disease aspect; the potential slamming from Trip Advisor; the 'putting it out of its misery' one), but I was distressed, cast down – as were Son and A – by the violent nature of the animal's death.

The whole thing cast a pall over the usual pleasure of eating.

Saturday 8th August

Happy! Last night at Asteri, I danced Cretan style for ages – with the group of experienced dancers. As we left, they asked me to come back for the final dance. I was immensely tempted, but it would not have been fair to the rest of the party.

Fabulous trip on the Barbarossa today: very rough (and loads of people were sick), but great fun!

The diary entry above marked the end of this fifth trip to Crete – and I have not visited the island since then. Having said that, I have plans – with various female friends I've made since moving to Glastonbury in 2016 – to hire a villa, for a week or ten days, and go back some day.

Beautiful view from Castello Taverna's terrace.

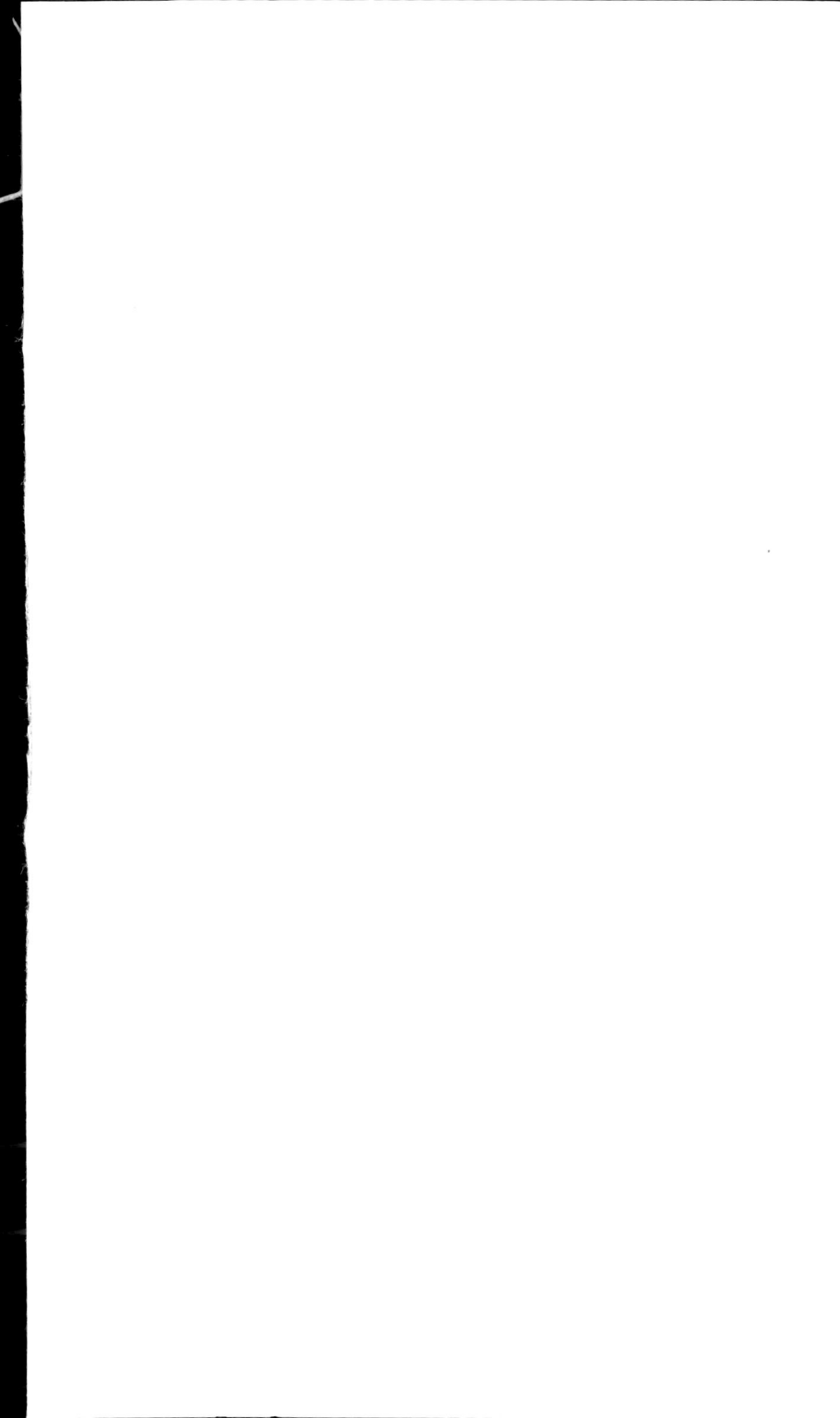

Printed in Great Britain
by Amazon